PENGUIN BOOKS

SO-ATY-295

TO UNDERSTAND IS TO INVENT

Jean Piaget was born in Neuchâtel, Switzerland, in 1896. His first interests were philosophy and zoology, and in 1918 he earned his doctoral degree at the University of Neuchâtel with a thesis on the distribution of the different varieties of mollusks in the Valaisian Alps. By then he had come to believe in the necessity of learning about intellectual processes, and he therefore turned to psychology, attending the lectures that Jung gave in Zurich. From 1919 to 1921 he studied in Paris, where he was associated with Théodore Simon, co-author of the Binet-Simon intelligence tests. He became professor of philosophy at the University of Neuchâtel in 1926, professor of psychology at the University of Geneva in 1929, and professor of general psychology at Lausanne University in 1937. His first book, *The Language and Thought of the Child*, was published in Switzerland in 1923. It was followed by many other works, all widely admired for their brilliant investigation of how children form the concepts of space, time, velocity, force, and chance. Professor Piaget is himself the father of three children, who have sometimes served as subjects for his psychological studies. His *Science of Education and the Psychology of the Child*, *Psychology and Epistemology*, and *The Child and Reality* are also available from Penguin Books.

TO UNDERSTAND IS TO INVENT

JEAN PIAGET

To Understand Is To Invent

The Future of Education

PENGUIN BOOKS

Penguin Books Ltd, Harmondsworth,
Middlesex, England
Penguin Books, 625 Madison Avenue,
New York, New York 10022, U.S.A.
Penguin Books Australia Ltd, Ringwood,
Victoria, Australia
Penguin Books Canada Limited, 2801 John Street,
Markham, Ontario, Canada L3R 1B4
Penguin Books (N.Z.) Ltd, 182–190 Wairau Road,
Auckland 10, New Zealand

"Le Droit à l'éducation dans le monde actuel" ("The Right to
Education in the Present World") first published in *The Rights of the Mind*
collection "Rights of Man" (UNESCO) 1948
"Où va l'éducation?" ("A Structural Foundation for Tomorrow's Education")
first published in "Prospects," quarterly review of education (UNESCO) 1972
This English-language edition first published in the United States of America
by Grossman Publishers 1973
Viking Compass Edition published by The Viking Press 1974
Reprinted 1975
Published in Penguin Books 1976
Reprinted 1977

"Le Droit à l'éducation dans le monde actuel"
and *"Où va l'éducation?"* copyright © UNESCO, 1948, 1972
English-language translation by George-Anne Roberts
copyright © The Viking Press, Inc., 1973
All rights reserved

LIBRARY OF CONGRESS CATALOGING IN PUBLICATION DATA
Piaget, Jean, 1896–
To understand is to invent.
Translations of Où va l'éducation and of Le droit à l'éducation dans le monde
actuel.
Includes bibliographical references.
1. Education—1945–2. Piaget, Jean, 1896–3. Education—Philosophy.
I. Piaget, Jean, 1896– Le droit à l'éducation dans le monde actuel.
English. 1976. II. Title.
[LA132.P513 1976]   370'.9'04   76-49924
ISBN 0 14 00.4378 0

Printed in the United States of America by
Kingsport Press, Inc., Kingsport, Tennessee
Set in Bodoni Book

Contents

Contents

TO UNDERSTAND IS TO INVENT

A STRUCTURAL
FOUNDATION FOR
TOMORROW'S
EDUCATION[1]

THE STRUCTURE OF OUR ESSAY FOLLOWS THIS plan: After a brief introduction which sets forth the condition of actual problems attending the recent trends in education, we will attempt to develop some thoughts on the future. These are in two areas. First, we will take as our example the teaching of sciences, in which field, it seems to us, the problems are presently the most urgent and the foreseeable reforms are the most complex. Then, drawing from those considerations, we will devote a brief section to reflections on some general questions.

Retrospective

From the quantitative point of view, the large and constantly growing number of schoolchildren has

[1] This article was written for a series of studies prepared for the International Commission on the Development of Education, at UNESCO.

resulted in a situation everyone is familiar with. On one hand, with the raising of the school-leaving age, greater educational equality for girls and boys, and State financial assistance (scholarships, etc.), there is more fairness in the educational opportunities offered to the young today, as is apparent from the constant and sometimes disturbing increase in the number of university students. But on the other hand, as this explosion in student numbers has not been accompanied by a much-needed social upgrading of the teaching profession at the secondary and particularly the primary level, the result has been a shortage of schoolteachers. This has led to the employment of substitutes and created a problem with regard to academic qualifications.

Nevertheless, an effort has been made to diversify curricula, particularly in vocational and technical areas, which is an improvement, and a number of steps have been taken to improve students' orientation by making it possible to change from one section to another, especially at the beginning of secondary school. The "orientation courses" have been very useful in this respect, but in spite of the worth-while work of educational psychologists, the value of the orientation and selection procedures remains an open question. The role and importance of examinations is a sore spot in education that does not always readily respond to treatment.

Statement of the problem

But from the qualitative point of view, the only one that interests us here, a series of more or less new trends has become apparent in the various countries leading present-day movements. Thus, an attempt to reform preschool education, sadly neglected up to now, is being made in several of them, in particular the United States. The main idea is that kindergarten for underprivileged children should offer them ethically and intellectually stimulating surroundings in which the atmosphere and above all the abundant and diversified material employed will compensate for the shortcomings of their family life and arouse their curiosity and energies. As to the methods used to direct all this, they fluctuate between two extremes and reflect two opposite currents in contemporary psychology. One is characterized by use of conditioning: establish and reinforce by practice and action a certain number of motor or verbal associations that are considered essential to knowledge to be acquired later on. The other by an appeal to the spontaneous activity of the child itself in the direction of a cognitive organization that prepares for the mental operations normally appearing at about age seven to eight. Inspired by the psychological research of the Geneva school, sometimes well interpreted (like the educational achievements of Allmy, Kamii, H. Furth, and so on in the United States) but sometimes also rather naïvely and unsatisfactorily, these applications may develop in a number of ways. We shall return later to what can be expected from the beginnings of cognitive activity—in regard to adequate observation of objective phenomena—as an introduction to the teaching of the sciences.

In line with what has been said above, the following changes can be seen at the primary level in certain countries (once again, the United States in particular). A few years ago the main trend, especially owing to the widespread influence of psychoanalysis, was carefully to avoid frustrating the developing child in any way. This led to an excess of unsupervised liberty which ended in generalized play without much educational benefit. A reaction has taken place in the direction of a chaneling and strengthening of cognitive activities. And here the opposition between the two extremes is even clearer. It results from the differences in the psychological convictions held.

The role assigned to conditioning, particularly under the influence of Skinner, has led to the ideal of programmed instruction through progressive associations mechanically arranged ("teaching machines"), and the enthusiasm for this approach in some circles is well known, although it is moderated by the cost of the apparatus required. Its fundamental defect is that it is based on a most inadequate psychology, which as the distinguished linguist N. Chomsky has conclusively shown, is unable rationally to account for the learning of languages. Programmed instruction is indeed conducive to learning, but by no means to inventing, unless, following S. Papert's experiment, the child is made to do the programming himself. The same goes for audio-visual methods in general. Too many educators have sung their praises, whereas in fact they may lead to a kind of verbalization of images, if they only foster associations without giving rise to genuine activities. The rods or colored numbers of Cuisenaire–Gattegno may sometimes give the students scope for performing a constructive operation, but frequently they, too, fail, owing to substitution of a figurative for an operational activity. This is why they have been abandoned in certain Swiss cantons, where they had been imposed by the State as unfailing remedies for difficulties encountered in learning arithmetic.

In many cases these rods have been replaced by the "multi-base arithmetic blocks" of Dienes, a mathematician and teacher whose long experience in education has enabled him to grasp this basic fact (confirmed, moreover, by my own psychogenetic research): the comprehension of elementary mathematics depends on the formation of qualitative structures (number, for instance, appears psychologically as a synthesis of the inclusion of classes and serial order), and the more the preliminary formation of the logical functions is facilitated, the greater the receptivity to mathematical instruction at every level. This fact obviously coincides with the present general tendency to introduce the "new mathematics" (theory of wholes, ten groups, etc.) at the most elementary levels. It represents an important advance. Later I shall try to examine the psychological reasons for its success, for the contents of this new teaching method must be brought into relation with structures and functions that are spontaneously active in the child's mind.

Mention should also be made of a series of experiments in science instruction carried out in Boston, Massachusetts; Illinois, and California by physicists and psychologists interested in elementary instruction who attempted to impart an understanding of certain simple physical phenomena to primary school—sometimes preschool—children by means of devices operated by the children with as much scope for spontaneity and active participation as possible.

Methodological trends

In closing this review section, I should point out that psychological research on the development of the intelligence and cognitive structures has made considerable progress in recent years, but that it remains divided into three tendencies of quite different significance as regards their educational application.

The first, remaining loyal to venerable Anglo-Saxon traditions, continues to pursue an empirical associationism that would assign a purely exterior origin to all knowledge, deriving it from experience or verbal or audio-visual representations controlled by adults.

The second is characterized by an unexpected return to factors of innateness and internal development (this to a great extent owing to the influence of the linguist Chomsky, who affirms the existence of an "innate fixed core"—despite the necessarily psychogenetic processes of transformation he acknowledges in grammar—which determines the basic structures of language; e.g., the relation of subject to predicate). Here education would mainly consist in training an innate "reason."

The third tendency, which is decidedly my own, is of a constructivist nature (attributing the beginnings of language to structures formed by the pre-existing sensory motor intelligence). It recognizes neither external preformations (empiricism) nor immanent preformations (innateness), but rather affirms a continuous surpassing of successive stages. This obviously leads to placing all educational stress on the spontaneous aspects of the child's activity.

Prospects for the future

As one of the questions with which educational authorities in different countries are most concerned is the proportionally small number of students choosing a scientific as opposed to a liberal arts career, it is obvious that this is one of the key problems that modern education must solve. It is no less evident that the problem will not be solved simply by the automatic interplay of economic forces. Society may need many more specialists in the most varied scientific fields than it has at present; economists may constantly insist on the earnestness of the shortages; students may well be informed from time to time of the fewer openings for liberal-arts graduates as opposed to the sure career opportunities awaiting those with adequate scientific training: these factors are far from being able to alter the educational orientation of students and

11

undergraduates. Some parents, for instance, continue to believe that knowledge of Latin is a more effective open-sesame than any other subject. Thus, it appears that in order to bring education into line with the needs of society, it would be necessary to undertake a complete revision of the methods and aims of education, rather than continue to be satisfied with simple appeals to common sense.

Science teaching

It is apparent that this reorganization would involve not only specialized training in the various sciences (mathematics, physics, chemistry, biology, etc.), but also more general questions, such as that of the role of preschool education (ages four to six); that of the true significance of active methods (which everyone talks about but which few educators effectively apply); that of the application of child and adolescent psychology; and that of the necessarily interdisciplinary nature at every level of the subjects taught as opposed to the compartmentalization still so widely prevalent both in the universities and secondary schools. Thus it is absolutely necessary to broach these questions as soon as we begin to discuss the scientific training of the young.

Starting with the basic psychological data, there is an essential fact in contradiction with what is generally admitted. Many people accept that there exist obvious differences of aptitude among individual students which increase in importance with age: if some students are plainly more gifted for mathematics or physics, etc., others will never achieve more than mediocre results in these fields. Having studied the development of the logico-mathematic functions in children for many years, I went on to study, with B. Inhelder at first, the education of elementary physical laws, then, in our International Center for Genetic Epistemology— with the constant assistance of several distinguished physicists—the development of notions of physical causality between ages four to five and twelve to fifteen.

More than 120 detailed investigations were made of the manifold aspects of this highly complex matter (problems of the transmission of movement, heat, etc.; composition of forces and vectors; changes of state in matter; dynamic movement and work; linearity and distributiveness, etc.). With the exception of a few girls who were not unintelligent, but simply lacked interest in these questions, we were unable to obtain any systematic data showing the existence of special aptitudes, as all the students from every age group with average or above-average intelligence made the same efforts and showed the same understanding. Of course, there exist retarded or advanced individuals, and those of below-average intelligence perform badly; but this is in every field, and not just in the sciences. Consequently our hypothesis is that the so-called aptitudes of "good" students in mathematics or physics, etc., consist above all in their being able to adapt to the type of instruction offered them, whereas students who are "bad" in these fields, but successful in others, are actually able to master the problems they appear not to understand—on condition that they approach them by another route.

What they do not understand are the "lessons" and not the subject. Thus it may be—and we have verified it in many cases—that a student's incapacity in a particular subject is owing to a too-rapid passage from the qualitative structure of the problems (by simple logical reasoning but without the immediate introduction of numerical relations and metric laws) to the quantitative or mathematical formulation (in the sense of previously worked-out equations) normally employed by the physicist. Nevertheless, we willingly admit certain aptitudes (once sufficient maturity is attained) that distinguish strictly deductive from empirical and factual minds, but even in mathematics many failures in school are due to this excessively rapid passage from the qualitative (logical) to the quantitative (numerical).

The very optimistic outlook resulting from our research on the development of basic qualitative notions, which ought to constitute the foundation of elementary instruction in the sciences, would seem to suggest that a fairly far-reaching reform in this area would help answer society's need for scientists. But this depends on certain conditions that are doubtless those of all intellectual training, although they seem to be particularly important in the various branches of scientific training.

The first of these conditions is, of course, the use of active methods which give broad scope to the spontaneous research of the child or adolescent and require that every new truth to be learned be rediscovered or at least reconstructed by the student,

and not simply imparted to him. Two common mis-
understandings, however, have diminished the
value of the efforts made in this field up to now.
The first is the fear (and sometimes hope) that
the teacher would have no role to play in these
experiments and that their success would depend
on leaving the students entirely free to work or play
as they will. It is obvious that the teacher as orga-
nizer remains indispensable in order to create the
situations and construct the initial devices which
present useful problems to the child. Secondly, he
is needed to provide counter-examples that compel
reflection and reconsideration of over-hasty solutions. What is desired is that the teacher cease being
a lecturer, satisfied with transmitting ready-made
solutions; his role should rather be that of a mentor
stimulating initiative and research.

Considering that it took centuries to arrive at
the so-called new mathematics and modern, even
macroscopic, physics, it would be ridiculous to
think that without guidance toward awareness of
the central problems the child could ever succeed
in formulating them himself. But, conversely, the
teacher-organizer should know not only his own
science but also be well versed in the details of the

development of the child's or adolescent's mind. The work of the psychogenetic experimenter is consequently indispensable to the effective use of active methods. Thus, in the era now opening up in education, closer cooperation than before is to be expected between basic psychological research (not "tests" or most of the devices of so-called applied psychology, which, in fact, like eighteenth-century medicine, attempted to apply what was not yet known), and systematic educational experimentation.

Two examples: Mathematics and experimental science

As regards teaching of the new mathematics, for instance, which constitutes such a notable advance over traditional methods, experience is often falsified by the fact that although the subject is "modern," the way in which it is presented is sometimes psychologically archaic insofar as it rests on the simple transmission of knowledge—even if an attempt is made (much too early as regards the student's manner of reasoning) to adopt an axiomatic form. Whence the stern warnings of eminent mathematicians such as Jean Leray in the periodical *L' Enseignement Mathématique*. What makes this situation so surprising is that if mathematics teachers would only take the trouble to learn about the "natural" psychogenetic development of the logico-mathematical operations, they would see that there exists a much greater similarity than one would expect between the principal operations spontaneously employed by the child and the notions they attempt to instill into him abstractly.

At the age of seven to eight, for instance, children discover by themselves assembling operations, the intersection of sets and Cartesian products, and at age eleven to twelve can discern sets of parts. The development of various forms or functions can be observed in very young children, and in many cases one can speak of "categories" in the sense of McLane and Eilenberg, which, although elementary or "trivial" in form, are no less significant as regards their educative value. But active intention and consequent practical application of certain operations are one thing, and becoming conscious of them and thus obtaining reflexive and, above all, theoretical knowledge are another. Neither pupils nor teachers suspect that the instruction imparted could be supported by all manner of "natural" structures. Thus one can anticipate a great future for cooperation between psychologists and mathematicians in working out a truly modern method for teaching the new mathematics. This would consist in speaking to the child in his own language before imposing on him another ready-made and over-abstract one, and, above all, in inducing him to rediscover as much as he can rather than simply making him listen and repeat. The educator/mathematician Dienes has made praiseworthy efforts in this direction, but an inadequate psychological knowledge makes his interpretation of the success of certain "games" or exercises he has devised somewhat too optimistic.

With physics and the natural sciences, one finds the situation completely different: the incredible failing of traditional schools till very recently has been to have almost systematically neglected to train pupils in experimentation. It is not the experiments the teacher may demonstrate before them, or those they carry out themselves according to a pre-established procedure, that will teach students the general rules of scientific experimentation—such as the variation of one factor when the others have been neutralized (*ceteris paribus*), or the dissociation of fortuitous fluctuations and regular variations. In this context more than in any other, the methods of the future will have to give more and more scope to the activity and the groupings of students as well as to the spontaneous handling of devices intended to confirm or refute the hypothesis they have formed to explain a given elementary phenomenon. In other words, if there is any area in which active methods will probably become imperative in the full sense of the term, it is that in which experimental procedures are learned, for an experiment not carried out by the individual himself with all freedom of initiative is by definition not an experiment but mere drill with no educational value: the details of the successive steps are not adequately understood.

In short, the basic principle of active methods will have to draw its inspiration from the history of science and may be expressed as follows: to understand is to discover, or reconstruct by rediscovery, and such conditions must be complied with if in the future individuals are to be formed who are capable of production and creativity and not simply repetition.

The way to renewal

CULTIVATING THE EXPERIMENTAL MIND

But there is a problem in regard to the adequate training of the scientists and technicians of the future by cultivating the experimental spirit. No doubt it is not peculiar to the understanding of physical phenomena, although some educators are already concerned with it in this respect, and it will doubtless become more and more urgent in all education based on psychology. In order to understand certain basic phenomena through the combination of deductive reasoning and the data of experience, the child must pass through a certain number of stages characterized by ideas which will later be judged erroneous but which appear necessary in order to reach the final correct solution. Thus, in attempting to explain the transmission of movement through a row of stationary, contiguous billiard balls, when the first is struck and only the last rolls, it is not till about age eleven to twelve that a child reaches the hypothesis of an internal transmission through successive shocks and vibrations, and admits that each intermediate ball has effected a slight molar translation: previously even when the intermediate balls were held motionless, by the pressure of a finger, for instance, the subject continued to believe they had moved, etc.

Many similar examples could be cited. Should everything be done to correct the child, or should the idea of active methods induce us to respect the succession of these approximations both in regard to their errors and their educational value? Future systematic educational experiments will have to decide, but for my part I believe there is every advantage in respecting these stages (on condition, of course, of knowing them well enough to be able to judge of their usefulness). It should be noted that a distinguished physics professor, F. Halbwachs, who in his *Outline* of elementary microphysics has adopted a similar point of view at the university level, justifies it by referring to the work of our Center of Genetic Epistemology. Unlike most authors, he begins with traditional concepts and gradually brings them into line with contemporary ideas, so as to facilitate the gradual assimilation of concepts which otherwise might remain partially incomprehensible.

All in all, the problem under discussion amounts to this: should passage from one stage of development be accelerated or not? To be sure, all education, in one way or another, is just such an acceleration, but it remains to be decided to what extent it is beneficial. It is not without significance that it takes man much longer to reach maturity than the other animals. Consequently, it is highly probable that there is an optimum rate of development, to exceed or fall behind which would be equally harmful. But we do not know its laws, and on this point as well it will be up to future research to enlighten us.

PRESCHOOL EDUCATION AND EXERCISING POWERS OF OBSERVATION

In continuing, by way of example, this investigation of probable future trends in science instructtion, let us first consider the increasing importance that will doubtless be attributed to preschool education. From the psychological point of view, the years from four to six (and even more so those from two to four, although we still lack systematic knowledge of them) may be described as "preoperational" in the sense that the subject is still unable to handle reversible operations (addition and subtraction, converse propositions, etc.) and consequently to discover simple constancies of quantities, matter, weight, etc., when sets of discontinuous elements (preservation of sets) or continuous objects change their form.

On the other hand, during these years the child already achieves what can be called a semilogic: one-way functional variations, qualitative identities (but not quantitative ones in their reversible form $\pm\ 0\ =$ "nothing has been added or subtracted"), etc. Leaving aside their limitations and relying on the positive aspects of these early attempts at establishing relationships, it appears possible to provide even at this level a kind of propaedeutic to scientific instruction which, for the rest, remains to be more extensively developed at the primary level. This propaedeutic would consist in exercising the powers of observation. And the importance of this activity should not be underestimated, as research has shown that at the preschool level perceptions are not only approximate and incomplete, as is obvious, but in many cases are also distorted by the preconceived ideas of the subject. Thus, in the case of a sling made of a ball attached to a string which the child whirls around and then throws into a box, it has been found that the action is performed successfully at age four to five after several tries, but its description is systematically distorted. The action itself is successful: the child releases the ball sideways, its trajectory being tangential to the circumference of the circle it described while being whirled. But he maintains that he released the ball either in front of the box or at the point of the circumference nearest to it, or even from in front of himself, as if the ball pursued a straight line from himself to the box, first passing through the diameter of the circle described by his arm.

The reason is first of all that in his eyes the action consists of two separate actions: whirling, then throwing (and not throwing alone). Second, it is usual to throw a ball into a box in a straight line perpendicular to the box. What is particularly curious is that although the action can be successfully executed at age four to five, a good description of it cannot usually be given before age nine to eleven. The object and the action itself (hence, awareness of the latter) are doubtless perceived but are, as it were, "repressed" because they contradict the child's preconceived ideas. This is only one example from among many others.

It can be seen that practice in observation could be very useful: the phenomena to be described would be simple everyday examples of causality, the descriptions themselves of various kinds: imitation of the action (the easiest), its verbal description, a graphic representation (with the help of an adult, etc.). An American professor of physics, Karplus (University of California), considers these observation exercises to be so useful, even at the preschool age, that he has devised situations with two observers in order to instill at a very early age an understanding of the relativity of observation.

STRUCTURED INTERDISCIPLINARY RESEARCH

I should like to stress once again a major question that concerns the secondary and university levels in particular: it is that of the more and more interdisciplinary nature of research in every field. At present, future researchers are ill-prepared in this respect, owing to instruction which aims at specialization but which ends in compartmentalization— the reason being a failure to understand that all thorough specialization necessarily involves relationships between many fields. It is a problem that concerns both the general epistemology and methodology of the sciences, but it seems clear that the future of the teaching of the sciences will depend more and more on their epistemology, something of which there are already many indications.

The explanation of the compartmentalizing of the sciences is to be sought in positivist prejudices. For a point of view which considers that only observable data count and that description and analysis suffice for the detection of the laws in operation, it is inevitable that the various fields should appear separated by clear and even fixed boundaries, inasmuch as the latter depend on the diversity of the categories of data, which are themselves dependent on our subjective apprehensions and objective instruments of observation. When, however, in violation of the rules of positivism (and in fact they are constantly violated, even when some authors, although their number is dwindling, endorse them in their prefaces) an attempt is made to explain phenomena and the laws governing them instead of limiting oneself to their description, the boundaries of the observable are necessarily overstepped, inasmuch as all causality depends on necessary inferences—i.e., on deductions and functional structures that cannot be reduced to simple facts.

Causality, indeed, consists of a combination of production and conservation, as to logico-mathematical operations, except that in physics the latter are attributed to the objects themselves, which are thus transformed into "agents." Then it is no longer the phenomenon or datum that is the basic reality but rather the underlying structure—reconstructed by education—that accounts for the phenomena observed. And because of this the boundaries between the disciplines tend to be effaced, for the structures are either shared (as in physics and chemistry) or interdependent (as will doubtless prove to be the case with biology and physicochemistry).

In view of which it is obvious that if the teaching of the sciences is to adapt to the conditions of scientific progress and form creative rather than imitative minds, it should stress structuralism, which with its interdisciplinary vision is gaining more and more acceptance and support. There is mathematical structuralism with the theory of groups and "categories," etc., physical structuralism with its indefinite extension of the attributes of the systems to explanatory models representing the intersection of the objects themselves; biological structuralism, with its problems of equilibration or self-regulation, even if the connections between cybernetic models and the structures that can be mathematically formulated are still obscure, etc. Nor should we forget the structures of the mind which, although studied by psychology, are to be brought into relation with all the preceding ones.

From the educational point of view, this is a highly complex state of affairs, promising for the future, but unsatisfactory as regards today. For although everyone talks of interdisciplinary needs, the inertia of established systems—i.e., those that are outdated but not yet eliminated—simply tend to create a multidisciplinary situation. This amounts to increasing instruction, inasmuch as all specialization requires support from the neighboring fields, but leaves it up to the student to make the syntheses himself. What is needed at both the university and secondary level are teachers who indeed know their subject but who approach it from a constantly interdisciplinary point of view—i.e., knowing how to give general significance to the structures they use and to reintegrate them into over-all systems embracing the other disciplines. In other words, instructors should be sufficiently penetrated with the spirit of epistemology to be able to make their students constantly aware of the relations between their special province and the sciences as a whole. Such men are rare today.

New relations between human and natural sciences

These few observations on the future of the teaching of the exact and natural sciences have bearing on a situation which, although of particular importance to the development of our societies, is nevertheless typical, inasmuch as the same problems are to be found in one form or another in all branches of learning.

The first lesson to be drawn from current interdisciplinary trends is the need to look closely at the future relations between the human and the natural sciences and the resulting necessity of finding a remedy for the disastrous consequences of dividing university instruction into "schools" and secondary schools into "departments," both of them separated by airtight compartments. From the theoretical point of view, psychology, considered a science of man, is connected without a break to biology and animal psychology or zoological ethology, whereas mathematics, classed among the natural sciences, is one of the most direct products of the human brain. The theory of information which came from the human sciences is just as useful to thermodynamics as the latter is to data processing and linguistics. The same goes for the theory of games which came from economics, etc.

From an educational point of view, it goes without saying that a general lowering of the barriers should be striven for as well as the opening of a generous number of side doors which would allow university as well as secondary-school students to pass freely from one section to another and give them the choice of many combinations. But it would also be necessary for the minds of the instructors themselves to become less and less compartmentalized, something that is often harder to obtain from them than from their students.

No centralizing discipline

Furthermore, it should be remembered that among the branches of learning classed as liberal arts, there is one which has always offered itself to every synthesis at both the secondary and university level and which many persons, unfortunately not always the best informed, still consider specially qualified to serve as a clearinghouse and headquarters for interdisciplinary relations: this is philosophy, of which a growing number of scientists are becoming distrustful—for reasons which will appear later— but which many biologists even now summon to their assistance as soon as they have understood the inadequacy of a certain archaic mechanism that was recently rife once again in their science. The delicate position of philosophy arises from the fact that whereas logic, psychology, and sociology have already left it, today mathematical, physical, and psychogenetic (etc.) epistemologies are being worked out, whose amalgamation will easily constitute the epistemology of tomorrow. It then becomes a question of knowing whether education will maintain the excessive privileges of philosophy in the future or whether liberal education will finally set out on the road to scientific structural-ism.

Structuralism is all the better adapted to fur-thering the development of the "human" branches of science because of its strong linguistic traditions, its success in social anthropology and certain schools of psychology, not to mention the many cybernetic and other models feeling their way in these sciences and increasing in the economic sec-tors. The result for education is that an increas-ingly large place must be reserved for new points of view—interdisciplinary by nature—like those that are being developed today by psycholinguis-tics, decision theory, economy, psychology, sociol-ogy, etc. This, however, does not mean more class hours at the secondary level, but rather a reorgani-zation of present curricula in the sense of a system-atic broadening of outlook, there being nothing to keep language teachers from acquiring sufficient linguistic knowledge to be able to give a broader scope to the study of grammar, or history instruc-tors from exposing the more general tendencies revealed by the evolution of civilization, rather than confining themselves to the succession of bat-tles and dynasties.

*Rediscovering the truth and practice of the
experimental mind*

But the problems that remain in the specifically
liberal branches are how to make sufficient room
for two fundamental elements of scientific education in the training of the young. These elements
are: (a) the genuine "activity" of the students,
who will be required to reconstruct, or in part rediscover, the facts to be learned; and (b) above all,
individual experience in experimentation and related methods. Of course, neither Latin nor history
can be reinvented, nor is it possible to make experiments (in order to "see for oneself"—i.e., of an
heuristic nature, or to verify explanatory hypoth-
eses) with Greek civilization. On the other hand, if
we have begun to understand the stages of development of the logico-mathematical operations or
causality in the minds of students in their partially
spontaneous manifestations, we do not yet have
comparable knowledge of the mechanisms that give
rise to linguistic structures and compel the understanding of historical facts. From the point of view
of psychopedagogical research, this constitutes a
series of still-unsolved problems, regardless of

whether their solutions will resemble those mentioned above.

As for educational practice—i.e., the need to introduce both liberal arts and science students to experimental procedures and the free activity such training implies—there are two possible solutions, neither excluding the other. The first, which seems to me indispensable, consists in providing mixed curricula with science classes (this is, moreover, already a general practice) in which the student can carry out experiments on his own. The second (which I believe should supplement the first) would mean devoting some psychology classes (within the framework of "philosophy" or future general epistemology) to experiments in behavioral psychology or psycholinguistics, etc.

Teacher training and team research

Two general problems remain to be considered. The first concerns teacher training, which indeed constitutes a question fundamental to all future educational reforms, for as long as it has not been satisfactorily answered, it is idle to set up ambitious curricula or construct fine theories about what should be achieved. It is a twofold question. First of all, there is the social problem of upgrading the teaching profession at the primary and secondary level, for the public does not estimate its services at their true value (hence widespread disaffection and teacher shortages), which constitutes one of the major threats to the progress and even survival of our ailing societies. Then comes the intellectual and ethical training of teachers, a very knotty problem inasmuch as the better the teaching methods imparted, the more difficult the task of the teacher. Better methods require of him highly specialized knowledge of his subject as well as of the student, plus a true vocation for his profession. There is only one solution: full university training for teachers at every level (for the younger the students are the more difficult the teacher's task, if it is taken seriously). This would follow the example of the training of doctors, etc. Such training is particularly necessary in order to ensure the acquisition of adequate psychological knowledge by both primary and secondary schoolteachers.

Finally, with regard to the future forms of the university, which will be just as responsible for the training of teachers as for other specialists, it is obvious that if the fatal role of the schools is to be reduced, mobile interdisciplinary groups of all kinds will have to take their place (for example, biology plus psychology plus linguistics or mathematics plus physics plus epistemology, etc.). But these combinations will remain inoperative as long as two basic principles and all their consequences are not applied: (a) a close union of training and research, the students being associated with the latter right from the start (otherwise they will run the risk of not understanding the already established science); (b) team research which is not supervised by a single professor but by representatives of neighboring fields working closely together (for instance, psychology and logic, etc., in spite of the difficulties attendant on such collaboration. These are not insurmountable as our experiments in Geneva have shown).

THE RIGHT TO EDUCATION IN THE PRESENT WORLD

Article 26 of the Universal Declaration of Human Rights voted by the United Nations* reads as follows:

1. Every person has the right to education. Education shall be free, at least in the elementary and fundamental stages. Elementary education shall be compulsory. Technical and professional education shall be made generally available and higher education shall be equally accessible to all on the basis of merit.

2. Education shall be directed to the full development of the human personality and to the strengthening of respect for human rights and fundamental freedoms. It shall promote understanding, tolerance and friendship among all nations, racial or religious groups, and shall further the activities of the United Nations for the maintenance of peace.

3. Parents have a prior right to choose the

* Adopted by the General Assembly, December 10, 1948.

kind of education that shall be given to their children.

Thus the obligations of society to educate the individual have been outlined, but certain social goals of education were emphasized as well: in particular, the obligation to combine the development of the individual with respect for other individuals. Finally, the role of the parents has been raised. It is to these diverse points of view that we will address ourselves successively in the commentary that we have been asked to make on this declaration.

The author of these lines is by no means a professional educator, but rather a psychologist led by his research to study the problems of the formation of man. It is thus in the spirit of the most objective psychological and sociological investigation that he would like to emphasize the urgency of the questions brought up by the present state of education.

1

"Every person has the right to education."

DEVELOPMENT OF THE HUMAN BEING IS THE RE-
sult of two groups of factors: the heredity and
biological adaptation factors, on which the evolution of the nervous system and elementary psychic
mechanisms depend, and the transmission factors,
or those of social interaction, which begin at the
cradle and which play an ever increasingly important role during the course of growth, in the constitution of mental life and behavior. To speak of a
right to education thus means first to ascertain the
essential parts played by social factors in the very
formation of the individual.

Only some kinds of lower animal groups are
entirely ruled by the play of instincts—that is,
hereditary dispositions remain internal to the individuals themselves. Already in higher animal
groups the achievement of certain behavioral
forms, exclusively instinctive or seemingly innate,
require the intervention of external social trans-
missions in the form of imitations, and of training
—in short, an education of the young by the mother

or father. For example, a Chinese psychologist has shown how the hunting instinct of small cats separated from their mother does not develop as well as when the same patterns of behavior are reinforced by maternal stimulation and example. But, in animal life, family life is short, and the beginnings of education that it encompasses remain quite limited. In the case of the more gifted anthropoids, the chimpanzees, connections between parents and their young cease after several weeks, and at the end of the first year the offspring is recognized by its mother in only one case out of five.

The essential difference between human and animal societies is that the principal points of man's social conditions—the technical means of production, language with its body of ideas whose very composition it permits, customs and rules of all sorts—are no longer determined from the inside by built-in hereditary mechanisms, ready to be activated in contact with things and relations: these behavioral patterns are acquired by external transmission, from generation to generation, by education, and develop only through multiple and differentiated social interactions. Since the time when men began to speak, for example, no language has been hereditarily fixed, and it is always through an external educational action of the familial surroundings on the young child that he learns his language, so well described as "mother tongue." Without a doubt, the potentialities of the human nervous system allow such an acquisition, while those of anthropoids do not, and the possession of a certain "symbolic function" is a part of these internal factors which society has not created, but which it utilized. However, without external social transmission (that is in the first place educational), the continuity of collective language remains practically impossible. Such a fact demonstrates from the beginning the role of this formative condition, insufficient in itself, but strictly necessary for the mental development that is called education.

Now, what is true regarding language—means of expression for collective values—is also true for these values themselves, as well as the rules applicable to them, beginning with the two most important systems of values and standards for the later adaptation of the individual to his surroundings: logic and ethics. For a long time it was believed that logic was innate to the individual and be-

longed, in fact and by right, to that "human nature" which common sense considered existent
prior to social living. From this idea, still commonly
held in the seventeenth and eighteenth centuries
(and to which common beliefs and concepts remain
attached), comes the principle that "logical faculties," etc., are "natural," and even by themselves
"natural" in contrast to the artificial products of
collective living. Descartes regarded "common
sense"—that is, the faculty of reasoning logically
—as the most widespread thing in the world, and
Rousseau founded his entire pedagogical system on
the contrast between the congenital perfections of
the individual and the later deviations due to social
living. These are the ideas that have inspired the
doctrines of traditional schooling: man, being pre-
formed in infancy, and with individual development composed solely of a realization of innate
faculties, with the role of education thus reduced to
simple instruction, it becomes only a question of
"furnishing" or nourishing capabilities that are
already formed, and not of forming them. It suffices, in a word, to accumulate knowledge in the
memory, rather than conceiving of the school as a

center of real (and experimental) activities carried out in common, so that logical intelligence may be elaborated through action and social exchanges.

Logic is never innate to the child. The clearest result of a body of research, encompassing not only the verbal thought of the young, but also their practical intelligence and the concrete operations through which they construct their classifications, their ideas of number and space, order and quantity, movement, time, and speed, etc., has brought forth evidence that certain reasonings held to be logically necessary, beginning at a certain mental level, are foreign to the earlier intellectual structures.

As a concrete example, all normal children, from seven to eight years old, will accept that, if two glasses of different shapes A and B contain the same quantity of water, and if two glasses B and C also contain the same amount, then the amount in A and C are equal, even when glasses A and C are of much more dissimilar shapes than A and B or than B and C. On the other hand, according to children from four to five years old, there is no reason to admit that amounts A and C are equal when it has been said that A equals B and B equals C, and there is also no decisive reason that the water remains the same although it changes containers.[1] In children from seven to ten or eleven years old, if they accept the reasoning A equals B, B equals C, therefore A equals C, when it is a question of a simple amount of water, they will doubt it when there exists a question based on a more complex premise (for example, of weight)[2] and, a fortiori, of arguments that are simply verbal (that is to say, without the manipulation of objects). Formal logic in the common adult sense of the term (I understand that to mean the capacity to reason according to such logic, as Mr. Jourdain was doing with prose without knowing it, and not the knowledge of such a discipline) does not really begin to be formed until eleven to twelve years old, and its complete achievement can take until the age of fourteen to fifteen years old.

Such facts as these profoundly modify classical terms of the pedagogical problem, and as a result, the meaning of the right to education: if

[1] Piaget and Szeminska, "Le Genèse du nombre chez l'enfant," Delachaux and Niestlé, chap. I.
[2] Piaget and Inhelder, "Le Développement des quantités chez l'enfant," Delachaux and Niestlé, chap. II.

logic itself is created rather than being inborn, it follows that the first task of education is to form reasoning. The proposition "every person has the right to education," as solemnly affirmed at the beginning of Article 26, means, therefore, in the first place, "every human being has the right to be placed in a scholastic environment during his formation which will enable him to build until completion the basic tools of adaptation which are the processes of logic." This formation is more complex than it seems, and special perspicacity is not necessary to be able to grasp that, in examining normal adult individuals who are representative of the honest, human average, the truly logical persons who are masters of their reasoning power are as rare as are the truly moral men who exercise their conscience with all their strength.

All of the above concerning the tools of reason may be more readily accepted than ethical formation—in theory, at least. Everyone would allow that, if certain inborn tendencies afford a human being the means with which to compose principles and ethical opinions, this elaboration presupposes the intervention of a set of particular social exchanges, first familial, and later of a more general nature. Everyone would recognize the formative role of ethical education (until a certain point) in contrast to tendencies that are simply hereditary in nature. But here again, and according to a parallel that comes to mind more strikingly with further analysis of the ethical formation and the intellectual formation of the individual, a question arises whether the external contribution expected from education regarding the completion of, and formation of, individual tendencies, congenital or acquired, can be restricted to a simple transmission of rules and of ready-made learning. Isn't this rather a question of imposing a certain obedience in accord with the intellectual obligation to retain and to repeat certain "lessons," or does the right of ethical education, as in the formation of the mind, mean a right truly to construct or at least to participate in the elaboration of the discipline that will obligate those very same persons who collaborated in this elaboration? In respect to ethical education, therefore, a problem in self-government arises, parallel to that of the self-formation of reason at the heart of an investigative collectivity. In any case, it should be underlined right away that the right to an ethical and intellectual education implies more than a right to acquire knowledge or to listen, and more than an obligation to obey: it is a question of a right to forge certain precious spiritual tools in everyone, which requires a specific social environment, not made exclusively of submissiveness.

Thus education is not only a formation but a necessary formative condition toward natural development itself. To say that every human being has a right to education is not only to suggest that every individual, assured by his psychobiological nature of achieving an already high level of development, possesses in addition (as is thought by individualist psychology, deriving from "common sense") the right to receive initiation from the society into its cultural and ethical tradition. On the contrary and much more profoundly, it is to affirm that the individual would not know how to acquire his most basic mental structures without some external influences, demanding a certain formative social milieu, and that on all levels (from the most elementary to the most developed), the social or educational factor constitutes a condition of development. Without a doubt, before three to four or six to seven years of age, according to the country, it is not school but rather the family that plays the educating role. So it could be replied perhaps that, while admitting the constructive role played by initial social interactions, the right to education, before everything else, concerns the child who is already formed by the familial milieu and ready to receive scholastic training; then it would no longer be a question of real formation, but only of instruction. But to dissociate the educational process in this way into two periods, or divide it into two spheres of influence, where only the first would be formative and the second would be restricted to the transmission of particular knowledge, would be to weaken once again the meaning of the right to education. Not only is the constructive scope of the latter diminished, but also school is separated from living: the basic problem is to make of school the formative milieu that the family tries to realize without always being able to achieve it sufficiently, and which constitutes the condition *sine qua non* of a full emotional and intellectual development.

Affirming the right of all human beings to education is to take on a far greater responsibility than simply to assure to each one reading, writing, and arithmatic capabilities; it is to guarantee fairly to each child the entire development of his mental faculties and the acquisition of knowledge and of ethical values corresponding to the exercise of these faculties until adaptation to actual social life. Moreover, it is to assume the obligation— keeping in mind the aptitudes and constitution that each person possesses—of not destroying or spoiling those possibilities that he may have that would benefit society first of all, or of allowing the loss of important abilities, or the smothering of others.

This is why the declaration of the right to education implies—if one has the desire to imbue it with a significance above the level of verbal declarations—the utilization of the psychological and sociological knowledge of laws of mental development, and methods and techniques adjusted to the innumerable basic principles that these studies provide the educator. It becomes a question, therefore, of determining by which methods this social milieu that is school will achieve the best formative results, and if this formation will consist of a simple transmission of knowledge and of rules, or if it presupposes, as we have already discussed, relationships that are more complex between teacher and student and among the students themselves.

We shall return to this point in referring to the "full development of the human personality" that is a postulate of our text.

For the time being we shall restrict ourselves to formulating the principle and to examining what its corollaries are from the point of view of society's obligations toward the child. This principle is that education is not simply a contribution that would be superimposed on top of the results of an individual development regulated in some inborn way, or that is accomplished by the family alone. From birth to the end of adolescence, education is one whole, and is one of two fundamental, necessary factors for intellectual and moral formation, so much so that the school carries a great responsibility regarding the final success or failure of the individual in pursuit of his own potential and adaptation to social living. In a word, the internal evolution of a person (according to the aptitudes of each one) only provides merely a certain amount of rough outlines that are capable of being developed, destroyed, or left in an untouched state. But these are only rough outlines, and only social and educational interactions will transform them into efficient behavioral patterns or destroy them totally.

The right to education, therefore, is neither more nor less than the right of an individual to develop normally, in accord with all the potential he possesses, and the obligation that society has to transform this potential into useful and effective fulfillment.

2

"Education shall be free..."

THE GAP THAT STILL SEPARATES EDUCATION AS IT now exists from what is implied by the right to education, if what we have just outlined is acceptable as a base, can be filled only step by step. First of all, there is a question of differentiating between the right to elementary education, which all countries recognize, although there are still obstacles to its actual application in many areas due to extreme difficulties, and the right to secondary education, which not all countries recognize as yet. Second, it is a matter of differentiating the right to attend an organized school and the right to everything that is encompassed in the term "full development of the human personality."

Thus, we shall begin with the school as it exists and with the right to receive an elementary education from it: "Education shall be free, at least in the elementary and fundamental stages. Elementary education shall be compulsory."

Elementary education is legally compulsory today in almost all countries. But we must not be deluded—such a legal reality does not imply that there is universal application of that law, for the number of schools and of teachers is insufficient in comparison with the number of school-aged children. Each year in quite a few regions a new contingent of young illiterates is added to the already considerable number of adult illiterates. That is why one of the first educational tasks that UNESCO undertook was the fight against illiteracy. A huge campaign for "basic education" was undertaken around the world in areas where modern civilization arrived only recently (certain regions of Asia and Africa, for example). There are also many countries civilized for a long time that have not yet solved the problem of illiteracy at school age. Moreover, in some areas the idea of elementary education is of interest to adults themselves, and some excellent progress has been made in several countries in the struggle against this type of illiteracy and in the perfecting of new pedagogical techniques adapted to this special goal. For example, everyone is familiar with the "school missions" established in Mexico (at the urging of the Director of UNESCO, Jaime Torres Bodet, when he was Minister of Public Education in that country), which spread elementary instruction to remote areas in the countryside and in the mountains.

But the problem of compulsory elementary instruction is coupled to a matter of social justice, or rather, of educational justice as well as social justice in particular instances. Compulsory elementary schooling (as well as its extension to adult illiterate groups) makes no sense until it is free of charge. All countries which have compulsory elementary education also accept the principle of its being free of charge. But it should be noted that there is a certain negative aspect of this principle: many other problems arise, some are extrinsic (free transportation for students living far away,[1] organization of free school cafeterias and even coatrooms, etc.), and some essential to teaching itself. Among the latter is the question of free school supplies.[2] All schoolwork requires some supplies, and the more active the methods, the more the supplies used increase in importance. It is clear that the student will take his activity more to heart

[1] "Dixième Conférence international de l'Instruction publique," recommendation no. 21, art. 6.
[2] "La gratuité du matériel scolaire," UNESCO and The International Bureau of Education.

if his work supplies and, above all, the result of
his efforts belong to him. In the traditional systems
of education it is only a matter of textbooks, note-
books, and paper, or of supplies required for drawing lessons and manual labor. But if as in the case
of active methods the role of textbooks diminishes,
the printing at school, the making of indexes and
files, the constructing of all sorts (graphic and
otherwise) requires an abundancy of supplies, and
the efforts that a student makes will always be
better when the product of his own work is and
will remain his own property. The idea of free
school supplies is still not sufficiently widespread,
in spite of growing tendencies in this direction all
over. Therein lies a question that is also as vital to
teaching as that of actual matriculation at school:
"The principle of free school supplies must be
considered the natural and necessary corollary to
compulsory schooling."[3]

If the solution to these questions is already
being sensed in many countries, the problem of
compulsory and free secondary education is, alas,
not in the same situation at all. Since the Third

[3] "Dixième Conférence international de l'Instruction publique," recommendation no. 21, art. 1.

Conference on Public Education convened by the International Education Commission in 1934, the international study of the "Extension of Compulsory Education" and of "Admission to Secondary Schools" has helped us to recognize some of the many obstacles that exist between these basic questions of educational justice or of "right to education," and the social questions connected with the organization of labor or professional structures; in short, the division of society into sociologically heterogeneous classes.

The situation is the following: either it is granted that all students have the right to a secondary education by uniformly fixing the upper and lower age limits for the educational process, and by giving families means to carry out this obligation, at which point there arises the question of the various possible types of secondary education and of the orientation of the students in different directions; or the compulsory character of secondary education is not recognized, and certain categories of students are channeled toward higher studies or simply toward diplomas that signify the end of secondary studies, while others give up all further scholastic activity to enter directly into apprenticeship, but then there is the problem of knowing what the criteria is that makes the selection, as well as what are the processes of orientation that form the basis of these divergent directions. In both cases, the same problem of scholastic orientation is found regarding any channeling toward a profession, more or less near or faraway. In both cases the solution depends on the same two factors: personal merit of the student and social and/or economic conditions of the family.

Under these conditions, can the right to secondary education be properly discussed, and what is the significance of granting this right? Paragraph I of Article 26 is entirely explicit on this point. Even if, for reasons depending on the economies of the countries concerned, education without charge is provisionally limited to the elementary stage, "technical and professional education shall be made generally available" and, above all, "higher education shall be equally accessible to all on the basis of merit." In other words, the right to a secondary education does exist, whatever the final career or profession of the student, and this right implies a professional preparation for all occupations, a channeling toward liberal careers—that is, access to universities and to other institutions of higher learning—dependent only upon the merit of the students and not on their conditions of class or race.

The complexity and seriousness of the problems thus brought out by such a declaration are easily understood: they can be grouped around three principles, each having the form of an antinomy:

1. From the social and economic point of view, it becomes a question of assuring the continuation of school attendance, independent of the economic conditions of the family, since the student's aptitudes and merit can be in conflict with his material situation.

2. From the point of view of transmitting collective ethics, it then becomes a question of reconciling adequate general culture with a professional specialization completed in time, since the conflict between these two demands increases with each scientific and technical advance.

3. From the point of view of the personal formation of the student, it becomes a question of assuring him a physical, intellectual, and ethical formation as full and complete as possible while

orienting him toward his own aptitudes. These aptitudes (which mean, by definition, that which dis-
tinguishes some individuals from others on the
same mental level) become more and more differentiated with age.

There is a basic fact that influences any solution to these three problems: that the normal intellectual and ethical development in the more
civilized societies is not completed until about the
age of fifteen. It is only at that age that it becomes
possible to uncover with some accuracy differentiating aptitudes of various individuals, while
before that age all orientation is hazardous and
risks neglect of important potentialities. Thus, if
we only think of the good of the student and of
society, it becomes necessary to assure a general
secondary education until that average age, leaving
the questions of professional channeling open,
allowing each student to acquire enough general
knowledge and also facilitating his definitive orientation at the end of this period of school
attendance.

This problem has sometimes been called that
of the "single school." A great deal of wasted discussion has revolved on this issue, since political

parties in certain countries have taken over this concept, naturally provoking opposition from other parties toward an idea that they themselves would have defended in another instance. This concept has been attacked and defended by the same parties at different moments in neighboring countries, while partisan struggles often give more lip service than real attachment to the idea. So we shall concentrate on the principle on which educators are tending more and more to rely. However diverse are the types of schools for children of eleven to twelve and fourteen to fifteen years old (beginnings of classic, scientific, or technical training with all their mixtures), it is important that the whole group of these schools constitute a single system or institution, so that change from one section to another is always possible, depending on results and failures along the way and of aptitudes that manifest themselves late (or, above all, of aptitudes that were not detected during secondary schooling). It is most important that such transfers or changes from one section to another not be considered as an exceptional measure, but rather as essentially a condition of good orientation.

If this principle is accepted, its application

requires a solution for the three problems outlined above, and it is then that the diversity of national organizational methods and the quite substantial gap that exists between reality and the desired ideal become apparent.

In the first place, there is the economic question, which dominates all others. Secondary education is already free in several countries (except for boarding-school costs, with a few rare exceptions), but it is certainly not generally so, and, except rarely, school supplies are not free. When the secondary school is free, it goes without saying that mere free tuition does not solve the financial problems that the family undergoes. There is the problem of the maintenance of the child, his inability to earn, of the distances that must be covered if the student lives far from the school, and, above all, his costs of living if he must stay in a particular town. Naturally, each of these problems recurs to a much greater degree on the university level.

Generally, the remedy most utilized has been the scholarship system, which is well known for the great help it has rendered and is still rendering to many gifted students, but it is obvious that the system is only a palliative since it is not sufficiently generalized, and it does not form a permanent collective guarantee supporting the right to secondary education in general. Many different formulas could be described. As a general rule, the amount of aid granted is determined simultaneously by the candidate's aptitudes and his family's economic situation. Numerous ways are thus utilized to facilitate detection of the gifted, and even sometimes to stimulate requests from some families who hesitate to ask, as if the granting of a scholarship represented some kind of exceptional subsidy, or even an act of charity. Therefore, on one hand, progress must be made to assure that grants in aid not be limited to specially gifted students only, but should also be applied so that all may enjoy a secondary education; and on the other hand, that a grant in aid is not an act of generosity on the part of the state, but is, rather, a response to a specific obligation of society.

The general effect of this situation has given rise in a variety of places to a growing movement for a real equality of access to secondary education, or of a "secondary school for all."[1] It has

[1] "L'Egalité d'accès à l'enseignement du second degré," UNESCO and The International Bureau of Education.

become evident that one of the most urgent problems of educational justice and of social justice today is underlined precisely here.

It goes without saying that a generalized secondary education does not mean a single and identical type of common orientation so that each and every student is aiming for admission to a university and a baccalaureate degree. Rather it is a matter of differentiating secondary instruction to a certain generalized extent so that the future manual laborer, future farmer, or future small businessman may find tools at the secondary level that are as useful to his later work as to the future technician or future intellectual, although these work tools may be quite different. It is here that the last two of the three problems outlined above arise: how to reconcile general culture with specialization, and the full rounded formation of the adolescent with his own aptitudes (two aspects of the same problem, in the sense of concerning the development of collective interests or values, and also that of the person himself).

Regarding the transmission of collective values, it becomes ever more obvious that the various activities of man form an indissoluble whole. For example, it is impossible to talk about the real life of a society without admitting the profound interdependence of scientific and technical ideas. It doesn't matter which comes first since they depend on each other in a continual historical process, of which the various aspects, even literary, of culture are equally dependent to different degrees (either through opposition to or avoidance of each other, as well as by direct dependence). The "general culture" which secondary education is to transmit to the student cannot, as is too often imagined, be restricted to an abstract formation (literary, scientific, or mixed) without roots in the structure and real life of the society as a whole, but must consolidate the different practical, technical, scientific, and artistic aspects of social intercourse into a more organic whole. It must bring the concept to an idea of the history of civilization in the widest sense of the term, and not only pertaining to the political and military events of history (rather the causes of related collective events than the consequences thereof). So it is not absolutely sure that, by extending secondary education to students aiming toward every profession, from the most manually oriented to the most intellectually, we must reach an impasse in regard to the necessary requirements for general culture and those of specialization. On the contrary, this "general culture" has much to gain by re-entrenching itself in reality and by being based on interaction between various aspects of social living; in short, by discovering and studying man such as he is and has always been, and not only as scholarly tradition has taught that he was. Beginning with secondary education, it becomes easy to conceive of certain teachings common to all the different divisions, as well as to others that are purely specialized.

The third problem is the most delicate of the three: how to reconcile general formation with specialization when it is a question of educating a particular individual and no longer that of transmitting a certain number of specific collective values, common or specialized, to an entire generation. This becomes a task that runs into basic difficulty since there are no two individuals alike. Practically speaking, in actuality, future orientation of the student is a matter that belongs to familial traditions and to economic class considerations. It is understood that the child born into a family of liberal professions will also pursue such a career under threat of losing social rank or caste, while the son of a peasant remains a peasant without exceptional aptitudes, etc. But if, as is solemnly declared in Article 26 of the new Declaration of the Rights of Man, and as is increasingly the general trend in civilized societies, access to the university should be on merit alone and secondary education should be generalized to all the other forms of professional channeling, then it becomes clear that the school is responsible for especially heavy and decisive duties—that of selecting and orienting not only for higher studies but also for all forms of professional activity imbued with equal dignity. Instead of evaluating only from the angle of future scholastic success, in the sense of being a step in the ladder toward only one goal—the university—the school is responsible for discovering and developing the most diverse individual talents.

The primary question is that of orientation: how to be able to diagnose aptitudes with sufficient objectivity at an age where they are not often prominent, and how to be certain of this diagnosis, which sometimes will involve the entire life and career of the student? Leaving aside for the moment the role of the parents, there are only two methods: examinations, strictly speaking, and analysis of work achieved during schooling, and these can be subdivided into two other categories. The examinations can, in effect, consist of either a school examination or a psychological examination conducted by a specialized person (the teaching personnel could itself also be instructed in the necessary psychological studies). The analysis of work could, on the other hand, be measured by scholastic results in the narrow sense of the word, which leads to some sort of test (weekly, monthly, etc.), simply generalizing the examination methods mentioned before. This analysis could be applied to activities per se, and partly spontaneous, on the part of the student, finding in this way methods of psychological examination that would indicate the general intellectual behavior of the student (instead of "tests").

Everything has been said about the value of scholastic examinations, and yet this veritable plague on education at all levels continues to poison—such terminology is not too strong here— normal relations between the teacher and the student by jeopardizing for both parties the joy in work as well as mutual confidence. The two basic faults of the examination are that generally it does not give objective results, and it becomes, fatally, an end in itself (for even admission examinations are always, first of all, final examinations: the admission examination to high school becomes an end for primary education, etc.). The school examination is not objective, first because it contains a certain element of chance, but mostly because it depends on memory more than on the constructive capabilities of the student (as if he were condemned never to be able to use his books once he was out of school!). Anyone can confirm how little the grading that results from examinations corresponds to the final useful work of people in life. The school examination becomes an end in itself because it dominates the teacher's concerns, instead of fostering his natural role as one who stimulates consciences and minds, and he directs all the work of the students toward the artificial result which is success on final tests, instead of calling attention to the student's real activities and personality. There is only one explanation for the maintenance of examinations, and it can be found in certain factors of social conservatism, and even sometimes of competition, which impose these protective devices on higher levels of the ladder, forcing their widespread generalization right down to the lower levels. When one discovers, for example, that the medical profession in some countries demands that ancient Greek be obligatory in schools for future medical students in such a way as to form a sort of artificial barrier, it becomes easier to understand motives that prevent the replacement of scholastic examinations by those for aptitude. It is not that such concerns have been primary reasons for examinations—this is better explained by the survival of the so-called initiation rites, and then by differences of opinion so often found in the history of social rites between the instrument and its use, etc. But to understand why such a system is maintained (when no one has any illusions as to its value), one must look for reasons buried in man's unconscious!

Attention to psychological methods of examination thus becomes a question of simple fairness and a necessary corollary to the right to secondary education. This has been understood in a growing number of countries, and there is presently a movement for the organization of such school psychological services,[1] as well as for the psychological training of the teachers themselves.[2] Psychologists have provided much material in the study of mental development, aptitude differential, and investigative methods that permit determination of level or aptitude. These methods may consist of either examinations by "tests" (capable of an indefinite number of variations at first, and primarily of setting up a correlation among them) or in more flexible and subtle procedures of analysis.[3] They are not perfect and are subject to continual revision and changes, as is true of all scientific methods. They do not replace in any way the analysis of actual results achieved by the student during his scholastic career (when this analysis is separate and distinct from school tests and is related to real work and not to memorized knowledge). But they are surely better than—and, in general, very different from—simple school exam-

[1] "Les Psychologues scolaires," UNESCO and The International Bureau of Education.
[2] "L'Enseignement de la psychologie dans la formation des maîtres."
[3] B. Inhelder. "Le Diagnostic du raisonnement chez les débiles mentaux," Delachaux and Niestlé.

inations, and they are intended to replace them more and more as admission tests.

The second orientation procedure is founded on actual work achieved by students during schooling. To the extent that the first classes of secondary school (from twelve to fifteen years of age) consist primarily in "orientation classes"—that is, that their organization makes it possible for divisions and passage from one division to another (after three, six, or twelve months)—the surest method of diagnosis and of prognosis is certainly that based on the observation of students and their real work. But it is a delicate method which, in our opinion, presupposes constant collaboration among the teachers, who are responsible for teaching, and the school psychologists, whose role is to follow the students individually in their successes and failures. It goes without saying that this method is only of value in relation to the very methods of education themselves. If the teaching consists of simply giving lessons and having them repeated in "recitations" or "tests," and of having them applied to some practical exercises that are always prescribed, the results obtained from the pupil will have hardly more meaning than in the case of any school examination, without considering the element of chance for the moment. It is only to the extent that the teaching methods are "active"—in that they form a greater and greater part of the initiatives and spontaneous efforts of the student—that the results obtained have meaning. This is a very sure and consistent method, and it could almost be called a kind of continual psychological examination, in contrast to the type of momentary sampling that tests constitute, in spite of everything. However, it should be repeated that fullest satisfaction can be obtained only through close association between pedagogical analysis and psychological analysis (the latter conducted by the school psychologist or by teachers who are sufficiently trained in psychological techniques).

Once oriented through this combination of psychological tests and a study of his individual activity, the student may definitively be directed toward the different branches of study where he will finish his secondary studies: various professional courses and/or preparation for the higher institutions.

3

"Parents have a prior right to choose the kind of education that shall be given to their children."

THE SCHOOL GUIDANCE THAT WE HAVE JUST DE-scribed is subordinated by line 3 of Article 26, to a restrictive condition that seems to go without saying: approval of the parents. Nevertheless, it is useful to point out that the whole history of human society shows a progressive reduction in the extent and rights of the family (from the "clan," from the "gens," from the patriarchal family, etc.), and a correlating extension of the powers of the state. It is also true that in education the full powers of the elders of the tribe, then of the paterfamilias, and finally of the parents in more recent centuries, have been more and more limited by an educational regimentation that has not always been to the child's advantage. Therefore, it is useful to analyze the actual situation in present circumstances where a group of new methods are simultaneously being proposed to the state and to the families.

First of all, it is the same with parents as with

everything else: there are excellent parents and others who are not so good, and it is useful to be able to protect the child against the latter's will. There are intelligent and well-informed parents and others backward and not so well endowed, who, for example, will hesitate to see a doctor and to follow his advice in case of sickness, and to whom it is impossible to speak of psychologists or of new pedagogy in education. . . . Above all, the problem is that of knowing how to act with parents of this type: good people, wanting only good for their offspring, but through ignorance or tradition-alism against all that really might be useful to them.

Most practitioners of the new kind of education have gone through the same experience; it is the parents who often are the greatest obstacle to the application of "active" methods. There are two combined reasons, and they are easy to understand. The first is that if one has confidence in known methods in usage for a long time there is some worry at the idea that one's own children might serve as experimental subjects, or "guinea pigs" (as if every change in program, book, or teacher in a traditional school were not an "experiment" as well!). The second is that the main preoccupation of parents on all levels of education and even of preschool familial education is that their offspring not turn out to be "backward." A baby must know how to walk at x months of age at the risk of becoming knock-kneed; a small child in nursery school must know how to read and count up to twenty at x years, while everything warns against artificially rushing, and advises the dedicating of this beginning period, precious to everyone, to the establishment of the most solid foundations possible. Now the multiple activities of manipulation and construction that are necessary to assure the practical substructure for the whole of later learning seem to parents like a luxury and a waste of time, simply delaying that solemn moment waited for by the entire tribe when the neophyte will know how to read and to count up to twenty! And so it goes at each new stage. . . .

Regarding the orientation of students at the secondary level, it goes without saying that there may be conflict between the counsel of the teacher or of the guidance psychologist and the parents' wishes. This does not mean at all that the parents are always insensitive to the efforts that the practitioners of orientation classes or the aptitude diagnostic specialists make to help them counsel their children. Still the problem exists concerning possible conflict between the will of the parents and the suggestions of the school or the orientation office. How can it be solved?

In spite of all these well-known circumstances, Article 26 is not reluctant to confer on parents the "prior" right to decide what type of education shall be given their children. That is because in all known societies, despite structural transformations in the family, it still remains a basic cog in the social structure. Therefore it can still always be called upon in the case of both the misinformed, or, rather, insufficiently educated parents, and the better informed, where parental education, if it can be called that, has been completed.

In this respect, if "every person has the right to education," it goes without saying that parents also have this right, and "prior right" as well. They have the right to be, if not educated, at least informed and even instructed about the better education that their children should receive. Two methods have been in use toward this end, and both merit serious support and encouragement.

In the first place, associations have been created and conferences on "familial education" have been organized with the goal in mind of attracting parents' attention to the problems of education within the family (emotional conflicts, both conscious and unconscious, etc.) and also to inform them on schooling and pedagogical questions in general. In some countries there are even some psychological and pedagogical publications directed to the layman on the same problems.

Second, movements for collaboration between the family and the school have been launched, especially where the new type of education is beginning to be important. They have been proved to be of inestimable value and beneficial to both sides. The school has everything to gain by knowing what the reactions of the parents are, and the latter find increasing advantage in being initiated into the problems of the school. A close relationship between teachers and parents thus leads to much more than mutual informational exchange: these exchanges are reciprocally advantageous and often lead to a real improvement in methods. In bringing the school closer to the life or the professional concerns of the parents and by giving the parents an interest in school affairs, a certain division of responsibilities is reached. In some countries parents' and teachers' associations together constitute the true source of inspiration for the new pedagogy, and in this way they carry out the hoped-for synthesis between the family and the school.

4

"Education shall be directed to the full development of the human personality and to the strengthening of respect for human rights and fundamental freedoms."

ARTICLE 26 OF THE UNIVERSAL DECLARATION OF
Human Rights is not restricted to affirming the
right to education. It specifies in a commentary as
important as this affirmation itself what the basic
goal of this education should be. It is obvious that
such a resolution implies a choice between the two
kinds of functions, public and private, that every
educational organization can be said to have; a
choice, or at least, a unifying postulate. From society's point of view, there is an immediate question
—is it necessarily the function of education to
develop the personality, or is it not, first of all and
even essentially, that of molding individuals according to a model of previous generations, capable of preserving collective values? In primitive
tribes the adolescent undergoes the ritual cere-
monies of initiation in an atmosphere of mystical
respect and emotional tension, sometimes for
months, and receives the sacred secrets that will
transform his free child's mind. With this knowl-

edge, he will be allowed to join the adult group, and it is clear that the principal goal of this education is not full development of the personality, but rather its opposite—submission to social conformism and total conversion to collective standards. One could ask if the traditional school with the submission of the students to the moral and intellectual authority of the teacher, as well as their obligation to absorb the sum total of learning necessary for success on final tests, does not constitute a social situation basically close to the aforementioned initiation rites and directed toward the same general goal: to impress the totality of commonly accepted truths upon the younger generations, which means the collective values and standards that have already assured the cohesion of previous generations. To state that education should undertake the full development of the personality is to declare that school should differ from such a classic model, and that harmony can exist between the formation of the person and his admission to collective life as a socially valuable human being as well.

But what is development of the personality? And by what educational methods can it be attained, since "full development" is never the end goal of all the known forms of education, but rather, it represents a demand that is contrary to the usual goals of conformist education and an ideal that must be reconciled with the collective goals of education.

The text of Article 26 gives no definition of "personality." However, it does state that its development is accompanied by a return to the respect for the rights and freedoms that belong to other personalities. Such precision seems almost tautological, but it is really important; an entire concept of personality could be defined by terming it a reciprocal "rapport." From a psychological point of view as well as from the sociological, it is essential to distinguish the individual and the personality. In the degree that the individual is self-centered, he creates an obstacle by his moral or intellectual egocentrism to the inherent relations of reciprocity that all evolved social living contains. Whereas, on the contrary, the part of an individual that is a "person" freely accepts some kind of discipline, or contributes to its creation, by voluntarily subjecting himself to a system of mutual "norms" that subordinate his liberty in respect to that of others. Personality, therefore, means a certain form of intellectual and moral conscience, as removed from the autonomy that is part of egocentrism as from the heteronomy of outside pressure, since it attains its independence by regulating it through reciprocity. It can be expressed more simply by saying that the personality is opposite to anarchy at the same time that it is opposite to any restraints since it is autonomous, and two such "autonomies" can only maintain reciprocal relations. To sum up, that "education shall be directed to the full development of the human personality and to the strengthening of respect for human rights and fundamental freedoms" is really to create individuals capable of intellectual and moral autonomy and of respecting this autonomy in others by applying the rule of reciprocity that makes it legitimate for themselves.

The pedagogical problem that is created by such a goal for education returns to the central question that lies at the heart of the entire school movement known as "active." Is it possible to form autonomous personalities by means of techniques that entail intellectual and/or ethical restrictions to differing degrees? Or isn't there a contradiction in terms since personality development really requires a free and spontaneous activity in a social milieu based on collaboration and not on submissiveness? It is appropriate to discuss this main problem facing all education. The sense and import of Article 26 depend entirely on its resolution. The right to education that it outlines so explicitly is not only the right to attend schools—but it is also, insofar as it pursues the full development of the personality, the right to find in these schools all that is necessary to the building of a questioning mind and a dynamic moral conscience.

A. Intellectual Education

Regarding the full development of the personality, can it be said that the methods of traditional schooling succeed in forming an active and independent mind in the child and in the adolescent?

The traditional school offers the student a considerable body of knowledge and gives him the opportunity to apply it to various problems or exercises. It "furnishes" the mind and subjects it to various ''intellectual gymnastics'' which are entrusted with strengthening and developing it. In cases where this type of learning is forgotten (and we all know how little remains of it five, ten, or twenty years after the termination of secondary studies), there remains at least some satisfaction in having exercised the intelligence; it is of little importance that all memory of the definition of cosine, rules for the fourth Latin conjugation, or dates in military history have been all but forgotten—having once known them becomes the important objective. Supporters of the active school reply that since so little learning is retained when it is learned on command, the extent of the program is less important than the quality of the work. A student who achieves a certain knowledge through free investigation and spontaneous effort will later be able to retain it; he will have acquired a methodology that can serve him for the rest of his life, which will stimulate his curiosity without the risk of exhausting it. At the very least, instead of having his memory take priority over his reasoning power, or subjugating his mind to exercises imposed from outside, he will learn to make his reason function by himself and will build his own ideas freely.

We do not believe that such a dispute can be solved by discussion alone or that pedagogy is the concern only of "authorized opinions." The art of education is like the art of medicine: it is an art that cannot be practiced without special "gifts," but one that assumes exact and experimental knowledge relating to the human beings on which it is exercised. This is not anatomical and physical knowledge like a doctor's, but psychological. This knowledge is no less essential, and the solution to questions on the active school or on the formation of the mind precisely depend on it in the most direct fashion. Psychological research on the development of rational operations and on the acquisition or construction of fundamental ideas provides data which seem decisively in favor of the active methods, and which require a much more radical reform of intellectual learning than many supporters themselves of the active school imagine.

Dependent as logical operations are on the nervous mechanisms that maturation allows to be set to work successively (the most recent parts of the human brain are not ready to function until toward the end of childhood), they are not constructed nor do they acquire their full structures except through certain exercise that is not verbal alone, but, above all and basically, is related to action on objects and on experimentation; properly so called, an operation is an action, but interiorized and coordinated to other actions of the same type according to precise structures of composition. On the other hand, these operations are not the attribute of the individual alone, but necessarily require collaboration and exchange between people. Thus, is it enough for the student to listen for years to lessons, in the same manner as the adult listens to a lecturer, for logic to be created in the child and adolescent? Or does a real formation of the tools of the intellect require a collective atmosphere of active and experimental investigation as well as discussions in common?

A representative example of this type of fundamental pedagogical problem is the teaching of elementary mathematics (in primary and secondary schools). It is here that teachers encounter the most difficulty, and where, in spite of all the qualities of their teaching, the nonactive methods that they are habitually compelled to use result in difficulties that are generally well known. It is notorious that in classes that are normal in other respects only a fraction of pupils absorb mathematics, and this fraction does not necessarily encompass all of the more gifted in other branches. Sometimes the comprehension of elementary mathematics comes to be considered as a sign of a special aptitude. The presence or absence of this mathematical "gift" is then considered to explain success and failure, whereas it could be asked whether they are not perhaps attributable to the classical method of teaching itself. Mathematics is nothing but logic, extending general logic in the most natural way, and constituting the logic of all of the more evolved forms of scientific thought. A failure in mathematics thus would signify a lack in the very mechanisms of the development of the intellect. Before making such a serious judgment on the probable majority of students and on the large majority of former students of our schools (for what remains of mathematics for most adults who are not specialized in science?), it must be asked if the responsibility does not lie in the methodology.

Something that is very surprising is the fact that everyone is convinced (by virtue of a system in which neither the school authorities nor the present teachers are the authors but which weighs heavily on the educational system) that to teach mathematics correctly it is enough to know it without having to be concerned with the way in which the ideas are established in the child's mind. Of course the teacher tries to be concrete, "intuitive," etc., and even to be inspired by mathematical history, as if the development of discoveries from Euclid to our time were consonant with the stages of the real psychological construction of the processes. But the teacher is not concerned with this psychological construction itself.

A series of ascertainments important to teaching can be made by studying psychologically the development of the spontaneous mathematical intelligence of the young child and the adolescent. In the first place, when the problems are posed without the child's perceiving that it is a question of mathematics (for example, during concrete experiments where questions of proportions, rules, and signs in the form of successive inverse operations, or of absolute velocities, or even relative velocities, etc.),[1] they are solved by the students with their general intelligence and not by special individual aptitudes (these are not to be excluded, but they do not play the preponderant role that it seems they do). In particular, students are frequently found who, though mediocre in lessons of arithmetic, prove to have a comprehensive or even inventive spirit when the problems are posed in relation to any activity that interests them. They remain passive and often even blocked in the school situation that consists of resolving problems in the abstract (that is, without relation to an actual need). Above all, they remain convinced of their inadequacy and give up beforehand, inwardly considering themselves defeated. Students who are thus reputedly poor in mathematics show an entirely different attitude when the problem comes from a concrete situation and is related to other interests. The child succeeds, depending on his personal intelligence, as if it were a matter of ordinary intelligence. A primary, basic result can be deduced from this: every normal student is capable of good mathematical reasoning if atten-

[1] Piaget. "Les Notions du mouvement et de vitesse chez l'enfant." Paris. University Press of France.

tion is directed to activities of his interest, and if by this method the emotional inhibitions that too often give him a feeling of inferiority in lessons in this area are removed. In most mathematical lessons the whole difference lies in the fact that the student is asked to accept from outside an already entirely organized intellectual discipline which he may or may not understand, while in the context of autonomous activity he is called upon to discover the relationships and the ideas by himself, and to re-create them until the time when he will be happy to be guided and taught.

Second, experiments that we have been able to carry out on the development of mathematical and physical ideas have demonstrated that one of the basic causes of passivity in children in such fields, instead of the free development of intellectual activity they should provide, is due to the insufficient dissociation that is maintained between questions of logic and numerical or metrical questions. In a problem of velocities, for example, the student must simultaneously manage reasoning concerning the distances covered and lengths utilized, and carry out a computation with the numbers that express these quantities. While the logical structure of the problem is not solidly assured, the numerical considerations remain without meaning, and on the contrary, they obscure the system of relationships between each element. Since the problem rests precisely on these numbers, the child often tries all sorts of computations by gropingly applying the various procedures that he knows, which has the effect of blocking his reasoning powers. This is again an example of the errors risked by believing in the innate logic of the child, whereas logic is built up step by step through his activities. When, on the other hand, the two types of factors are dissociated, one can advance more surely, all in attaining the true goal of mathematical learning—the development of the deductive capabilities. It is easy, for example, to give children from ten to twelve years old even complicated problems of velocities (composition of the speeds of two moving objects where one changes place with another or in relation to another, acceleration on an inclined plane, etc.) without numerical data and by bringing the reasoning power to bear on the simply logical relationships (on the more and the less and not on the "how much"— that is to say, in the way in which Aristotle reasoned on the problem of speed!). Freed from the necessity of computation, the child enjoys building actively all the logical relationships in play and arrives thus at the elaboration of procedural operations that are flexible and precise, often even subtle. Once these mechanisms are accomplished, it becomes possible to introduce the numerical data which take on a totally new significance from what they would have had if presented at the beginning. It seems that a lot of time is lost in this way, but in the end much is gained, and, above all, an enrichment of personal activity is achieved.

Third, psychological study of logical and mathematical ideas of the child has shown that a real and spontaneous development exists of these ideas, partly independent—not of exchanges with the social milieu, which is the necessary stimulant to all thinking, but of learning that, strictly speaking, is acquired at home or at school. Thus, as an elementary example, until a certain age the child thinks that an object that changes its shape (such as a ball of modeling clay) also changes its quantity of material substance, of weight or volume. It is through independent working of logical coordination that he arrives at the point where, disgarding these generally unsuspecting initial stages, he considers as necessary the maintenance of the quantity (toward seven to eight years old), of weight (nine to ten years old), and of physical volume (about eleven to twelve years old). It is equally true that the child builds by his own means his elementary geometric ideas (maintenance of distances, of parallels, of angles, perspective, construction of reference systems in relation to physical orientations, proportions, etc.)[1] without anyone's suspecting these logical transformations in the child's mind. This spontaneous intellectual elaboration is not only richer than can be imagined, but it also illuminates a very clear-cut law of evolution: that all mathematical ideas begin by a qualitative construction before acquiring a metrical character. In the area of space in particular, the child's representation is, in the beginning, less influenced than one might think by the metric relationships in play in perception. On the contrary, it comes from the type of relationships that mathematicians call topological, well before becoming

[1] See Piaget and Inhelder, "La Représentation de l'espace chez l'enfant," and Piaget, Inhelder, and Szeminska, "La Géometrie spontanée de l'enfant." Paris. University Press of France.

situated in the position of Euclidian geometry (this is otherwise of great interest to modern mathematicians). Therefore, an entire adjustment in the didactic methods in psychological data on real development remains to be made, and it is to be hoped that this point of view will considerably reinforce the appeals for independent activity for the child.

Fourth—and this is a summary of all the preceding—mathematics is taught as if it were only a question of truths that are accessible exclusively through an abstract language, and even of that special language which consists of working symbols. Mathematics is, first of all and most importantly, actions exercised on things, and the operations themselves are more actions, but well coordinated among themselves and only imagined instead of being materially executed. Without a doubt it is necessary to reach abstraction, and this is even natural in all areas during the mental development of adolescence, but abstraction is only a sort of trickery and deflection of the mind if it doesn't constitute the crowning stage of a series of previously uninterrupted concrete actions. The true cause of failures in formal education is therefore essentially the fact that one begins with language (accompanied by drawings, fictional or narrated actions, etc.) instead of beginning with real and material action. Mathematical training should be prepared, starting at nursery school, by a series of exercises related to logic and numbers, lengths and surfaces, etc., and this type of concrete activity must be developed and enriched constantly in a very systematic way during the entire elementary education, to change little by little at the beginnings of secondary education into physical and elementary mechanical experiments. On these terms, strictly mathematical education is grounded in its natural surroundings of equivalency to objects, and will give full scope to the intelligence which would have remained purely verbal or graphic.

Just to give one example: everyone knows the difficulty that secondary students (and even university students!) have in understanding the algebraic rule of signs—"minus times minus equals plus." This rule of signs is discovered in action by children of seven to eight, already under different qualitative forms. When a thin iron rod transversing three beads, ABC, is turned around a small screen (with the movements of the rod being visible, but not those of the beads), the child understands that the order ABC changes to CBA. He then understands that as soon as two turns around are completed the order becomes ABC again, that three rotations becomes CBA, etc. In this way he discovers, without knowing it, the rule of composition that states that two inversions in direction cancel each other. In other words, "Minus times minus equals plus." But when he reaches fifteen to sixteen years of age, he will not understand the algebraic computations, of which he will learn the existence, unless they appear to him as a continuation of actions of this type!

We have stressed this example of mathematics somewhat since there is no field where the "full development of the human personality" and the mastery of the tools of logic and reason which insure full intellectual independence are more capable of realization, while in the practice of traditional education they are constantly being hampered. There is nothing more difficult for the adult than to know how to appeal to the spontaneous and real activity of the child or adolescent. Only this activity, oriented and constantly stimulated by the teacher, but remaining free in its attempts, its tentative efforts, and even its errors, can lead to intellectual independence. It is not by knowing the Pythagorian theorem that free exercise of personal reasoning power is assured; it is in having rediscovered its existence and its usage. The goal of intellectual education is not to know how to repeat or retain ready-made truths (a truth that is parroted is only a half-truth). It is in learning to master the truth by oneself at the risk of losing a lot of time and of going through all the roundabout ways that are inherent in real activity.

If this must be brought out regarding the methodology of mathematics, how much more reason there is to appeal to activity in teaching languages, geography, history, natural sciences, etc. That is, in every field where knowledge of facts has no value except in relation to the processes of discovery that enable it to be absorbed.

Full development of the personality in its most intellectual aspects is indissoluble from the whole group of emotional, ethical, or social relationships that make up school life (we pointed out above this kind of emotional inhibition that so frequently blocks the reasoning power of students after some lack of success in mathematics). At first sight, personality development would seem to depend above all on emotional factors, and the reader might even have been surprised that to illustrate this idea of free development of the individual we began by logic and mathematics! In reality, education constitutes an indissoluble whole, and it is not possible to create independent personalities in the ethical area if the individual is also subjected to intellectual constraint to such an extent that he must restrict himself to learning by rote without discovering the truth for himself. If he is intellectually passive, he will not know how to be free ethically. Conversely, if his ethics consist exclusively in submission to adult authority, and if the only social exchanges that make up the life of the class are those that bind each student individually to a master holding all power, he will not know how to be intellectually active.

Moreover, do the so-called active methods, which are alone capable of developing the intellectual personality, necessarily require a collective milieu that is the molding element of the ethical personality as well as the source of organized intellectual exchanges? No real intellectual activity could be carried on in the form of experi-mental actions and spontaneous investigations without free collaboration among individuals—that is to say, among the students themselves, and not only between the teacher and the student. Using the intelligence assumes not only continual mutual stimulation, but also and more importantly mutual control and exercise of the critical spirit, which alone can lead the individual to objectivity and to a need for conclusive evidence.

The workings of logic are, in effect, always "cooperations" and imply a whole range of mutual intellectual exchanges and relationships and of both ethical and rational cooperation. The tradi-tional school recognizes only the social exchange that is connected with a teacher, who is a kind of absolute ruler in control of moral and intellectual truth over each individual student. Collaboration among the students and even direct communication among them are thus excluded from classwork and homework (because of the examination atmosphere and "grades" to be met). The active school, on the other hand, presupposes working in common, alter-nating between individual work and work in groups, since collective living has been shown to be essential to the full development of the personality in all its facets—even the more intellectual. An entire technique of "work in teams"[1] has been developed in many countries under different names. Here is only one small example. When we visited Decroly some time ago, we accidentally found a group of pupils studying a problem in analytical geometry in a back room, some in groups, some alone. In listening to their discussion, I could not help recalling that the few ideas I learned at the same age in that field (a branch that scared me then) were not due to any explanations by a comrade, but from explanations on the margin of school life, and they were a little irregular, while in the group I was observing, working together was the normal method!

B. Ethical Education

The problem of ethical education is exactly parallel to those we have been discussing regarding logic or mathematical training. Do we wish to form people who are subjected to the restraints of

[1] "Le travail par équipes à l'école," The International Bureau of Education.

earlier generations and traditions? If so, then the authority of the teacher is enough, and consequently also the "lessons" in ethics, with the system of rewards and punishments reinforcing this obedient behavior. On the contrary, do we not wish rather to form simultaneously free consciences and individuals who respect the rights and freedoms of others? It becomes evident that neither the teacher's authority nor the best lessons he can give on the subject suffices to engender living, dynamic relationships, comprised of both independence and reciprocity. Only a social life among the students themselves—that is, self-government taken as far as possible and parallel to the intellectual work carried out in common—will lead to this double development of personalities, masters of themselves and based on mutual respect.

Many pedagogical experiments show the results of self-government[1] when it has not been artificially imposed and hence contradictory, but rather when it corresponds to the spirit of the entire school. Moreover, a number of psychological investigations have led to detailed information

[1] "Le Self-Government à l'école," The International Bureau of Education.

on the respective influences of various relationships of authority and of reciprocity among adults and children, or among children themselves. These pedagogical experiments, which were already under way before World War II, have revealed that, in the tragic circumstances that many village urchins came out of after the war, there existed a truly comforting revival: perhaps these small groups, formed of children united by their common misfortunes, can provide us with the best and soundest reasons for having hope in a better future for humanity, since it is evident that there exists a possibility of renewal in a social atmosphere formed of affection and freedom (that is to say, not of obedience, but of responsibility freely assumed).

We have stated that the two correlative aspects of the personality are independence and reciprocity. In contrast to the individual who has not yet reached the state of "personality," and whose characteristics are to be oblivious of all rules and to center on himself whatever interrelations he has with his physical and social environments, the person is an individual who situates his ego in its true perspective in relation to the ego of others. He inserts it into a system of reciprocity which implies simultaneously an independent discipline, and a basic de-centering of his own activity. The two basic problems of ethical education are, therefore, to assure this de-centering and to build this discipline. But what are the means that the educator has at his disposal to achieve this double goal —means furnished either by the psychological nature of the child or by the relationships that are established between himself and other members of his environment?

Three types of feelings or emotional tendencies, capable of affecting the ethical life of the child, are found first in his mental constitution. In the first place, there is the need for love, which plays a basic role in development in various forms from the cradle to adolescence. There is a feeling of fear regarding those who are bigger and stronger than himself, which plays not a negligible role in his conduct of obedience and conformism, utilized in differing degrees by several moral educational systems. The third feeling is mixed, composed of affection and fear at the same time; it is the feeling of respect that all moralists have underlined as being exceptionally important in the formation or exercise of moral conscience. For some, respect constitutes a derivative emotional state, unique of its type—it would have other people as its object, like love or fear, but it would be attached directly to moral values or laws represented by these individuals. To respect a person returns thus to respecting the moral law in him (Kant), or the discipline he represents and applies (Durkheim). According to other authors with whom we ourselves are linked, respect, while capable of secondarily gaining higher forms, is, first of all, like the first two, a feeling of an individual toward an individual. It begins with the mixture of affection and fear that the small child feels toward his parents and for the adult in general (before conflicts and disillusions have colored these early attitudes).

The relationships between the child and the various other persons in his environment play a basic role in the formation of ethical feelings where the accent will be put on one of the three varieties of affective tendencies that have been outlined up to now. It is essential to understand that, if the child carries in himself all the necessary elements for the elaboration of an ethical conscience or "practical mind" as he does for an intellectual conscience or reasoning, neither one nor the other is given factors at the starting point of mental evolution, and both are built in narrow connection with the social milieu. The relationships that the child has with the people on whom he depends will therefore be, strictly speaking, "formative," and will not be limited to, as is generally thought, exercising more or less profound influences, but considered somewhat accidental in the construction of even the most elementary ethical realities.

One kind of relationship is that which engenders a feeling of obligation. Such is the case of the first exercises accepted and felt as obligatory by the small child. The striking and, on reflection, even surprising phenomenon is that of the baby who, hardly possessing a hold on the first words of his mother tongue, accepts orders and considers himself bound by them (whether or not they are carried out or transgressed, he feels himself guilty or embarrassed in relation to the adult); why does he accept such rules instead of ignoring them (as he knows how to do so easily when he is being told stories that bore him)? This acceptance is not simply the product of the stronger will. Fear of it alone does not obligate him to acceptance, but rather gives rise to a purely external (as well as purely self-seeking) obedience (to obey so as not to be punished, etc.). It still remains to be explained that there is an inner acceptance and, as a result, the feeling of obligation. This is where the second condition intervenes and becomes one of the three given factors mentioned above regarding the spontaneous tendencies of the child. The instruction or order is only accepted and only engenders a feeling of obligation if it comes from a person who is respected—in other words, one who is the object of both affection and fear at the same time and not only one of these two emotional states. In this way, the small child does not feel obligated to an order from a brother whom he loves, however, or from a stranger whom he only fears, while orders from the mother or father make him obligated and this continues to be felt even if the child disobeys. This first type of relationship, assuredly the earliest in the formation of ethical sentiments, is capable besides of remaining at work during the entire childhood, and to outweigh all others, depending on the type of ethical education adopted.

But if the importance of this first stage of

ethical relations can be perceived, the inadequacies become apparent in the point of view that we are presently concerned with. The respect that a small child has for the adult, source of obedience and submissiveness, remains essentially unilateral since, if the adult respects the child, it is not in the same sense (the adult does not feel obligated to orders and instructions which he does not receive anyway, and would never accept). While it is unilateral, this initial type of respect is, above all, a factor of dependency. Doubtless the child discovers in growing up that the adult subjects himself —or at least endeavors to subject himself without always being able to do so, in fact—to the orders that he gives. The rule is thus sooner or later felt to be superior to those he respects. On the other hand, the child one day experiences a multiplicity of instructions, sometimes contradictory, and finds himself in the position of having to make choices and establish hierarchies. But, without a source of outside ethical behavior other than unilateral respect alone, he will remain what he was at the beginning—an instrument submissive to ready-made rules, and to rules whose origin remains external to the subject accepting them.

At the other extreme, in the interindividual relationships that are formative of ethical values is mutual respect.[1] It forms between two equal individuals or where all authority is abstracted, and it is still a mixture of affection and fear, but it has only that part of "fear" that is related to any lowering of prestige in the eyes of the other. Mutual respect thus substitutes for the heteronomy characteristic of unilateral respect, an independence necessary to its own functioning and recognizable from the fact that individuals obligated by it participate in the elaboration of the rule that obligates them. Mutual respect is therefore also a source of obligations; however, it engenders a new type of obligations which no longer impose only ready-made rules, strictly speaking, but also the method that creates them. This method is none other than reciprocity, understood not only as an exact balancing of good and bad but as the mutual coordination of points of view and actions.

What are the effects of these two forces, unilateral and mutual respect: this de-centering of the ego and building of an independent discipline,

[1] Piaget, "Le Jugement moral chez l'enfant," Alcan.

which we have recognized as necessary to the education of the ethical personality? They are easily perceived in exact parallel with what we stated above in regard to the education of the intellectual personality. Education, founded on authority and only unilateral respect, has the same handicaps from the ethical standpoint as from the intellectual standpoint. Instead of leading the individual to work out the rules and the discipline that will obligate him or to work with others to alter them, it imposes a system of ready-made and immediately categorical imperatives on him. In the same way that a kind of contradiction exists in adhering to an intellectual truth from outside (without having rediscovered and reverified it), so it can be asked whether there does not exist some moral inconstancy in recognizing a duty without having come to it by an independent method.

In fact, many psychological principles have been gathered on this subject, utilizing widely varying methods. There are studies on the behavior of children, first subjected to authoritarian methods or placed in self-governing groups, then changed in environment, and before their adaption to the new conditions.[1] There is research on the development of ethical judgment in the child, analysis on emotional conflicts between children and parents, or the role of the "superego"—that is, the unconscious persistence of parental authority, etc. The results of these diverse investigations are convergent: discipline endured from outside either snuffs out the whole ethical personality or obstructs more than favors its formation. It produces a kind of compromise between the external layer of obligations or of conformist behavior, and an "ego" always centered on itself, since no free and constructive activity has allowed it to experience reciprocity with others. In other words, just as a pupil can recite his lessons without understanding them and can substitute verbalism for rational activity, so a child obeying is sometimes a spirit subjugated to an external conformism, but does not understand the real meaning or facts surrounding the rules he obeys, or the possibility of adapting them or making new ones in different circumstances.

[1] See work of the Lewin school (Lippit, etc.).

In studying how children of different ages conceive of lying and how they morally evaluate different types of lying submitted to their judgment, we have been struck by how much their reactions resemble (but in moral terms) some of their misunderstandings of an intellectual nature. So, to the child of less than seven to eight years old, it is much worse to lie to a big person than to a comrade (since the prohibition comes from the adults) and the gravity of a lie is measured by the objective or material falsehood of the affirmation and not by the intention to lie. To say in exaggeration that one has seen a dog as big as a calf is a "bigger lie" than to have falsely attributed a good grade in school to oneself, since the latter, in contrast to the former, could have been true and precisely because the "parents would have believed it!"). The standard of truth—accepted as obligatory before being understood, before being lived through real and mutual social experience—thus engenders a sort of "moral reification" (recalling the "objective responsibility" of early forms of juridical legalism). But the child, once thinking through the standard of truth, due to social interchange, experience, and reciprocity, becomes capable of very subtle evaluations on his subject.

The educational importance of mutual respect and of the methods founded on the spontaneous social organization of the children among themselves is precisely to permit them to work out a discipline where the necessity is discovered in action itself, instead of being received ready-made before being able to be understood. And this is why the active methods give an equally invaluable service in ethical education as in the education of the mind. They intend to lead the child to construct for himself the tools that will transform him from the inside—that is, in a real sense and not only on the surface.

The best proof that it is not merely a question of simple deduction or of theoretical psychology is the ever-enriching pedagogical experiment of self-government. Before World War II some trials were being carried out on a large enough scale to permit valuable ascertainments to be made. But it should be recognized that most of the tentative efforts of that time were inspired by the ideas of eminent educators more than by the necessities of life, which, in the eyes of the public, gave them an appearance of theory alone, or at least of exception, and related to especially favorable school circumstances (for example, the boarders at private institutions who had no financial difficulties or definite compulsory programs).

Between 1930 and 1935 we visited an institution that had none of these characteristics and that impressed us greatly: it was an establishment for young delinquents in an eastern European country, where the admirable man who directed it was audacious enough to have confidence in the children and adolescents he was in charge of to the point of putting the matter of house discipline in their hands and of giving the most exacting responsibilities to the most difficult. Two aspects of this experiment were particularly striking—the re-education of the newcomers by the social group of young people themselves, and the organization of the inner tribunal of the establishment whose functioning was performed entirely by the boarders. Regarding the first point, it can easily be imagined what impression the new arrivals must have had of an independent organization in which the house rules were imposed by the groups of comrades

themselves, and not by the adults. A child or adolescent who had been caught in the wrong, then
sentenced by a penal court, expected discipline of
exceptional severity and continual prohibitions.
But he found himself in the presence of young
people on the road to healing or to regeneration
(after having received the same sort of sentence)
and who formed an organized social group that
immediately welcomed him by giving him a work
assignment, obligations, and responsibilities. This
is not to say that, thus put into relation with equals
and not with wardens, the individual was instantly
transformed, and that his errors did not happen
again. But it is here that the most beautiful discovery of this brilliant educator appears: the
errors of one of the boarders, once they were in-
corporated into the community, were judged by a
tribunal made up exclusively of comrades and
named by them alone. The deliberations and
arrests of this astonishing court of justice were
kept in a logbook that we were able to see (with
the help of one of our assistants). There could be
nothing more fascinating for the psychologist than
this document, undoubtedly since destroyed during
one of the battles of Warsaw. The humanity,

understanding, and subtle evaluation of these adolescent judges had something very moving and heartening in them.

In this connection, we should point out that one of the most delicate aspects of ethical education and precisely where the greatest gap exists between the methods of independence or of reciprocity, which are the formative elements of the personality, and authoritarian methods, is exactly related to the problem of punishment. This problem is that of forms of punishment that are degrading to the person who administers them, and whose principle is felt to be totally unjust by the child even before he gets used to confusing their usage, and the actual deeds, with morally sound rules.

On the contrary, by resorting to reciprocity instead of authority, a way of building confidence instead of punishing is opened up which encourages the development of the moral personality more than any restriction or external discipline.

This very exceptional experience which we had the privilege of knowing between the two world wars has been repeated since on a large scale with abandoned children, orphans who were victims of the war, and children who had lived under such frightful circumstances that every appearance of any distinction between good and evil seemed to have disappeared. And this experiment has been carried out again in surroundings of varied pedagogical tendencies, whether with Soviet educators or Italian priests, "partisans" belonging to one clan or another, etc., and the results have been the same in every case, because the sociological laws of children's societies and the psychological laws of personality development are relatively constant (in contrast to the variety of relationships which differentiate the development of the child in various adult environments).

On the whole, whether it is a question of education of the mind and of intellectual functions, or of education of the ethical conscience, if the "right to education" implies that it envisions "full development of the human personality and . . . the strengthening of respect for human rights and fundamental freedoms," it is important to understand that such an ideal cannot be attained by any of the common methods. Neither the independence of the person, which is assumed by this development, nor the reciprocity that is evoked by this respect for the rights and freedoms of others can be developed in an atmosphere of authority and intellectual and moral constraints. On the contrary, they both imperiously demand a return, by their very make-up, to the "lived" experience, and to freedom of investigation, outside of which any acquisition of human values is only an illusion.

5

"Education shall promote understanding, tolerance, and friendship among all nations, racial or religious groups, and shall further the activities of the United Nations for the maintenance of peace."

THE PROBLEM OF INTERNATIONAL EDUCATION
raised by the above passage is one of the most
delicate that educators face. In contrast to the case
of ethical and intellectual formation where it
could be considered that the level attained by the
adult is superior to that of the child, and can therefore serve as example to present to students, the
current international situation cannot be regarded
as a model of perfection. The search for an adequate technique in international education should
at least start with a consideration of the difficulties
(which characterize the human spirit in general)
that rule the problem of relations between social
groups, and particularly the question of international relationships.

Such difficulties do not prevent some from
imagining that a special training, given in all
schools and related to the present international
institutions and their efforts to maintain world
peace, would be able to reinforce the spirit of

understanding among nations and would efficiently serve the cause of peace. There are no objections that can be raised against such attempts (for everything should be done toward such a goal, even risking inefficient procedures, or those not sufficiently disengaged from the partially verbal methods of traditional pedagogy) as long as there is no danger that they result in the opposite effect. Nothing would be more distressing than to leave students with the impression of too great a distance between the actual state of things and the ideal that is strived for, without their understanding the real reasons for this gap. Now, who really understands them?

Besides, we have not meant to say that all verbal teaching is useless either in the area of international education or in other areas. But it can be useful only when prepared by preliminary activity and given as part of a general attitude in circumstances of a social and ethical nature. If, as has been said, a lesson should be a response, it becomes necessary (regarding international education more than the others) that this response be preceded by spontaneous questions directly related to this activity and these attitudes.

129

A comparison will allow us to understand this. What is the best method to make a pupil a future good citizen (of his country, without yet speaking of the world)? Is it simply to give him, for a certain number of hours a year, a systematic course of "civic instruction" by describing to him bit by bit the different workings of national institutions that leave him still relatively indifferent, in spite of the eloquence or good will of the teacher? Or is it to graft such training onto the experience of self-government in the school so that the child knows by experience what an executive committee, a general assembly, and a court are, and can be interested in analogous institutions at a level he could never imagine without such analogies? We even maintain that if it should be necessary to sacrifice the teaching of "civic instruction" to the practice of self-government, the latter would produce better citizens than the finest lessons, and that if these lessons are given without social experience to support them, their practical results risk being of little worth (we are speaking here not as a teacher, but as an old student whose recollections are quite exact on this particular point).

How does the problem of international education differ from the questions of moral or even intellectual education studied above? The problems are somewhat similar, on a different scale perhaps, but this difference in scale is of such importance that even adults have, practically speaking, never been able to resolve the question of relationships between nations—that is to say, to educate each other internationally. The problems are, in effect, comparable, since when it is a question of intelligence, ethical formation, or international formation, the issue is each time to "de-center" the individual, to make him spontaneously give up his subjective or egocentric attitudes, and to lead him to reciprocity and (this is practically synonymous) to objectivity. Only it is relatively easy to coordinate the points of view of individuals on a question of pure intelligence (for example, of putting into relation perspectives of different observers), and still relatively easy to coordinate them concerning a moral conflict, but reciprocity and objectivity seem to become an insurmountable difficulty on the level of national feelings and in international life.

Two preliminary remarks should be made in

this regard. The first is that social reality, in general, and particularly the present international reality, are among the things we least understand. It is easier for us to talk about the movements of the stars and about physical and chemical phenomena than about social and international facts, which command our attention constantly. Contemporary social reality constitutes something new enough if it is compared with humanity's past history; every important event that happens in each of our national societies immediately takes on a universal character and reverberates on the whole world. Collective phenomena have changed scale, and the level on which they occur is one of complete interdependence. In spite of artificial attempts for national economic and spiritual self-sufficiency, there no longer exists in fact "national economies" any more than isolated internal politics, or even intellectual reactions and morals limited to a single group. Banal as this statement may be, it nevertheless corresponds to a state of affairs that, in truth, we have not succeeded in assimilating, and to which we are not yet accustomed. Without a doubt we easily perceive the causes—they are the technical and economic transformations since the beginning of this century. But two world wars have been necessary for us to become conscious of this interdependency of nations, as well as to realize at the same time how difficult it is to re-establish unity, or equilibrium, once it has been lost, and the narrow kinship of the conflicts that arise among nations and the internal conflicts of these nations themselves.

We are not adapted psychologically to our social state, and this is the basic fact we must begin with in order to construct an international education. And "we" means not only the masses of mankind lost in front of this universe of complex and interdependent relations; it is also even the men of state. As Valéry has pointed out so well in his "Regards sur le Monde Actuel," the contemporary man of state almost plays dice in international politics. Whatever the continuity of his line of conduct, when he is in possession of a political plan that extends beyond questions of immediate security for his country, he is led to feel his way, and often to contradict himself regarding the details of his actions, while their repercussions are unforeseeable.

We do not understand the present world

either morally or intellectually. We have not yet found the intellectual tool that will aid us in coordinating the social phenomena or found the ethical attitude that will permit us to control them by will and by heart. We are like the old Eskimo who was asked by an ethnologist why his tribe so piously preserved certain rites, and answered that he could not understand what was the meaning of that: "We preserve our old customs so that the universe will continue."

For primitive man, the universe is a great machine in unstable equilibrium where all is related to everything else (the social customs and physical laws are not differentiated one from another). If one removes even one of its pieces, even without knowing what purpose it has, the whole machine risks being thrown out of gear. The social universe is, for us, a little like what the entire universe is for this primitive man—we guess that there is a relative harmony, a global mechanism that works or deteriorates, and since we doubt, we preserve all that we can, at the risk sometimes of impeding precisely that good functioning.

The first task of the educator concerning the international problem is therefore to attempt to adapt the student to such a situation without hiding any of its complexity. It is to mold a spiritual tool in the mind of the child—not a new habit, or even a new belief, but rather a new method and tool that will permit him to understand and to find his way. In speaking of an intellectual tool we can refer to science, which is one of the most beautiful adaptations of the human spirit and a victory of the mind over the material world. Now, how has it succeeded? Not only by accumulating knowledge or experience. Far from that. It is in constructing an intellectual tool of coordination, thanks to which the mind has been able to put facts in relation to each other. That is what we require from a social point of view. It is not only to give the child some new knowledge of international institutions and realities, for they will not be useful for anything to him if, at the same time, an attitude *sui generis*, an instrument of coordination both intellectually and ethically valid on all scales and adaptable to the international problems themselves, has not been created.

Now (and this will be our second comment), the basic obstacle to progress in intellectual coordination and ethical reciprocity is none other than the more spontaneous and ineradicable attitude in every individual and even in the collective conscience: this is the egocentrism, both intellectual and emotional, which is found in every individual spirit in the degree that he is more primitive and not yet de-centered by social interactions. And it is the intellectual and emotional sociocentrism which reappears in every collective unit, depending again on the amount of "de-centering" that has been carried out. This is an attitude so naturally anchored in every consciousness that it is impossible to overcome it at one time by some sort of total conversion of these spontaneous tendencies, for it reappears, degree by degree, at each new conquest of coordination. This liberation is essential in relation to the "I" and the "We," and it demands a considerable moral and intellectual effort and assumes constant will power, and even sometimes a kind of heroism.

Science, which we invoked before, is there to show us how profoundly the egocentric attitude is rooted and how difficult it is to undo it by the brain as well as the heart. Thought has not succeeded in adapting itself to the outside world, and the human spirit has not become capable of foreseeing and explaining physical phenomena, except by freeing itself always first from the initial egocentrism. But this change of perspective has required centuries of labor.

This is what the history of astronomy has shown us with particular clarity. The sun, the moon, and the stars appeared to the first men just as they seem to young children: like small lights, situated at the height of clouds and of mountains, which accompany us as we go along with a fixed trajectory. Every child has thought one day that the moon was following him, and, according to several primitive societies, the course of the heavenly bodies is ruled by the movement of men (in ancient China, the Son of the Heavens insured the seasons by his moving about). The Chaldeans and the Babylonians made notable progress in freeing themselves from this initial egocentric vision and in understanding that the heavenly bodies have a regular trajectory which is independent of us. But this victory for objectivity still allowed a second form of egocentrism to survive and even grow: the earth conceived as a great plateau, then as a hemisphere, and finally as a sphere, retained its apparent position. Most Greek scholars still considered that the heavenly bodies revolved around this so-called center of the universe. Such a belief, of course, illustrated by Aristotle's system, is not comparable to that of the child who thinks the moon follows him. Still, it proceeded from the same type of illusion and did not weigh any less on the history of ideas till the time when Copernicus and Newton understood the exact relations of the earth and the solar system. The Copernican revolution can be considered a most striking symbol of the victory of objective coordinations over the spontaneous egocentrism of the human being. However, once more, egocentrism recovered in a new and more refined form: to coordinate his system of the universe, Newton allowed for a time and space absolutely identical in every point of the universe to that of our clocks and terrestrial meters! Still two more centuries were required for Einstein to teach us the relativity of time and space, depending on velocity, and to construct a tool of coordination much more subtle still than that of classical mechanics, waiting to be surpassed in turn.

Throughout this evolution it can be seen that, if at each new level human thinking has come to disengage itself from a particular form of egocentrism, seemingly primitive or naïve after the fact, it is to fall once again each time into a more refined egocentrism, which again impedes complete objectivity. From a social point of view, it is, a fortiori, the same thing; the "de-centering" of the "I" or the "We" or of their symbols or of their territories is still hampered by more obstacles. Each time we liberate ourselves from this "I" or "We" in favor of a collective cause that inspires us only with altruism and generosity, we become the victim of some new and insidious deviation, still more tenacious as it is unconscious. Who can, seeing that, overcome the social or international problems, when national egocentrism, the egocentrism of class, the egocentrism of race, and many other forms more or less powerful, divide our spirit and tax it with a whole gamut of errors in stages between the simple delusion of perspective and of fallacies that are due to collective inhibitions?

It therefore becomes obvious that international education cannot be restricted to adding one more course to the ordinary courses that will simply bear on present international institutions or even on the ideal that they represent and defend.

First of all, it is the entire teaching that must become international, not only history, geography, and living languages, fields where the interdependence of nations is more than evident, but also those of literature and science, where the common efforts of the whole human race, as well as the role of social and technical conflicts, are too often neglected.

It is only with such a spirit permeating the whole of teaching that one can expect this spirit of understanding and of tolerance toward all racial and religious groups which we have mentioned in our text, for how can the history of civilization, of literature, of science be taught from an international angle without becoming the enemy of all intolerance?

Above all, it is only by starting with a group of active methods, with first priority being investigation in common (work in teams), and the social life of the students themselves (self-government), that the study of national and international attitudes as well as the difficulties of their coordination can achieve some kind of concrete significance. And this from two points of view:

First, international life is the theater of the

same conflicts of reciprocity and the same mis-understandings of all social intercourse on an entirely different level. Judgments that one country has on other countries, the astonishing myopia that permits whole nations to reproach in others (with all sincerity) attitudes that characterize their own behavior to an equally great degree, the inability to put oneself in perspective with regard to opinions that are different from one's own, etc., are all common phenomena on all levels, and to understand their importance on the international plane it is essential to have discovered them through a "lived-in" experience.

Second, as soon as a social life is organized among the students themselves, it becomes possible to extend it in the direction of international exchanges or even of study groups that have international problems as their object. Interschool correspondence, mutual help clubs for the youth of other countries, international travel groups (exchanges of students at vacation time or even during class time), and many other initiatives already begun between the two world wars are active procedures in which real achievements have been obtained. But one could also conceive of study groups related to international education at the secondary level, with research in common on one or another aspect of international life as a goal. The usefulness of these groups would be great, provided they were granted complete freedom, especially complete freedom from criticism. For example, one could conceive of a group of secondary students trying to establish (without engaging the responsibility of the teacher, and with a free exchange of ideas) through a comparison of newspaper articles or of radio broadcasts what are the multiplicity of points of view on the same event and what are the difficulties of an objective history. It is not impossible that the day when the pupils learn to think and to read newspapers (or listen to the radio) in such a spirit of discernment and criticism, peoples themselves will hesitate to allow themselves to be led exactly like schoolchildren—we want to say like the schoolchildren of the "Old Regime," those who never benefited from the transformations in teaching that are postulated in Article 26.

Sources

"A Structural Foundation for Tomorrow's Education" was written in 1971 for the International Commission on the Development of Education, at UNESCO.

"The Right to Education in the Present World" appeared in *The Rights of the Mind* collection "Rights of Man," published by UNESCO, Librairie du Recueil Sirey, Paris, 1948.

Index